WE KNEW WE WERE AT WAR

Women Remember World War II

To Paula — Best wishes Peg George

Also by Margaret Hewitt George

A George/Yerk Genealogy 1752-1994
(with Wilmer Krause Yerk)

A Krause Genealogy—Descendants
of Jacob and Magdalena Krause 1741-1994
(with Wilmer Krause Yerk)

Never Use Your Dim Lights—Not Even in the Fog
A Political Journey

WE KNEW WE WERE AT WAR

Women Remember World War II

by Margaret Hewitt George

To the Hewitt family

My parents - Margaret and Charles Hewitt

My brothers - Charles and George Hewitt

and to

Glenn – always

ISBN 0-9777944-0-7

Published in the United States

To order copies:
Margaret H. George
133 Progress Drive
Doylestown, PA 18901
215-345-0522
www.PegGeorge.com
E-mail: info@PegGeorge.com

Second Printing
Printed in the United States of America

Cover and interior design by Foster Winans, Prose & Pictures, Inc.

Posters were obtained from the Northwestern University Library World War II Poster Collection web site and can be viewed in color at the following address: http://www.library.northwestern.edu/govpub/collections/wwii-posters

Library of Congress Control Number: 2006922069

✪ TABLE OF CONTENTS ✪

✪ ALPHABETICAL INDEX ✪

Preface

Imagine you are visiting a museum. Instead of viewing magnificent pieces of art, you enter a series of galleries filled with stories, photographs, and World War II posters. Stop in front of one of these stories and spend a few minutes experiencing life in the early 1940s, a time of momentous change.

In the first gallery, you will learn what life was like here at home in the United States as you read about food rationing, blackouts, tar on your bathing suits, and knitting bandages for servicemen. Meander through other galleries to learn about women at work, women in the military, women waiting for husbands to return from war and, finally, to women who experienced firsthand the horrors of war in other lands.

At the end of your visit, you will have transported yourself back into those difficult years when we all knew we were at war.

For those who remember, please share your stories with your children and your grandchildren. Together we can help keep history alive.

Acknowledgements

A very special thanks to all the women and their family members who shared their memories. Without them, there would have been no book.

Thanks also to those who helped in the preparation of this book: Heidi George, Barry George, Lorrie Cartee, Bill Hewitt, Elizabeth Miller, Jackie Gentile, Nancy Thomas, Sandy Werkheiser, Fran Warwick, David Gilleece, and Jim Demerest of Oneida, Ltd.

Introduction

While clearing out folders in the fall of 2005, I discovered a paper I had written for a course—"The Philosophy of Feminism"—that I had audited 14 years earlier at Gwynedd Mercy College near Philadelphia. My paper was about the United States between the years 1935 and 1945, including World War II, from the perspective of a teenaged girl living in eastern Pennsylvania.

Seven years later, in February 1998, my husband and I were taking a course at an Elderhostel in Florida: "The History of Modern Germany." My journal entry for February 12 reads, "Our professor attributed to United States industry the greatest part in winning World War II." This made me think that when I was a high school student working eight hours a day, six days a week at Westinghouse, I had as much to do with our victory as the soldiers and sailors. My life was not on the line, but all of us women working here at home played a crucial role. The professor noted that Hitler and his advisors had no idea Americans would have the will and discipline to create such a powerful war machine.

After taking the course, I occasionally asked a female friend or relative to tell me what she was doing during World War II. Some of these stories I wrote down and others I stored in my memory, not knowing what I might do with them, but feeling the need to preserve them.

The war in Iraq and Afghanistan spurred me on to gather more stories from the past, and I decided it was time to make them available to the public. Thus, the book you hold in your hands.

Our country is at war now, yet only those families with loved ones in the service or otherwise directly involved are paying the price. During World War II, everyone from schoolchildren to grandparents was involved or directly affected in some way. We all knew we were at war.

Many of the entries in this volume are in the women's own words. Some have been provided by family members, and others are the result of conversations I had with the subjects. In several instances, I have condensed excerpts from books or other personal histories. In all cases, I had great cooperation, enthusiasm, and gratitude from the participants.

I hope you find this slice of our history as fascinating and moving as I have.

—Margaret Hewitt George
Doylestown, Pennsylvania
March 2006

Women and their families

Mary Caughey McCaw

Mary had a brief career in advertising before settling near Philadelphia, Pennsylvania, and raising three children. Her leadership and interests have been directed toward troubled adolescents, criminal justice, and the arts.

"Pull down the blinds, Mary. Close the door to the dining room. Oh, and get the little white radio and plug it in on the counter next to the stove."

Mother said we were preparing for a mock air raid, a test to see if our town was ready in case the Germans came.

"I don't think the Germans will find us here," I scoffed.

Perhaps I was wrong. We lived in a small town thirty miles northwest of Pittsburgh, Pennsylvania, within range of a number of steel mills, which could have been prime targets. My father worked for a company that manufactured the rivets, used by "Rosie the Riveter" to hold our aircraft together.

An aunt of mine had had a boarder for several years, a German man who worked in the mill. In the late 1930s, he packed his things and quietly left. We were convinced he had been a spy.

I lowered the blackout blinds and closed off the kitchen as the family sat around the enamel-topped table in the middle of the room. It was the only room where we could keep the lights on during an air raid test. I finished my Latin homework. Mother and Daddy read the evening paper. My sister Margaret worked on the sweater she was knitting, and my brother Rick studied his lines for a play.

The siren wailed, and we knew that Mr. Shields, the Air Raid Warden for our block, was out patrolling the darkened street. Joe, our next-door neighbor, was pretending to be injured and the first aid crew would find him lying in the gutter, a tag attached to his shirt that said he had a chest wound so the trained medical volunteers would know the appropriate treatment to administer. The same routine was taking place on many blocks between the hill and the river. Of course, we could not witness this drama because we were ordered to stay inside to await the all-clear signal, which would allow us to resume our usual activities.

I lowered the blackout blinds and closed off the kitchen as the family sat around the enamel-topped table in the middle of the room.

The late Sunday afternoon in December, 1941, when we learned of the Pearl Harbor attack, Margaret, Rick, and I had been making fudge. It hardened in the pan after we pulled it off the stove and ran into the living room to listen to the radio. The sun had already set, and darkness surrounded us as President Roosevelt spoke. Mother had a worried look on her face. "I've had a feeling we'd soon be drawn into this," said Daddy. Mother nodded and rose to go upstairs. "Better get ready for church," she called. We usually went to church on Sunday evenings, and this surely was no time to miss the prayer service.

I was fifteen, a sophomore in high school. My brother was finishing college as a day student and my sister was also living at home, taking the train daily to Pittsburgh where she was the receptionist at the H. J. Heinz Company. How oblivious I was to the potential upheaval that war would bring to

The Air Corps song was the one which made my blood surge as we sang, "Down we dive zooming to meet our thunder, at `em boys, give `er the gun. Give `er the gun!"

lives all over the world. For me, there was actually something romantic about the country going to war as I read newspaper accounts of the boys barely older than I who were being drafted. They came home on leave a few months later, handsome in their uniforms, their hair sheared short, swaggering with a grown-up confidence they had acquired during basic training.

One day, Margaret told us she had learned at work that Heinz was converting part of its food plant to the manufacture of gliders for the war effort. My brother reported that some of the fellows in his college class had enlisted. He was hoping to finish his education before being drafted.

Rick's number came up shortly after he graduated, and he was sent to Georgia for basic training. In the window of our sun parlor, Mother hung a red, white and blue flag with one blue star on it indicating that a person in our home was serving in the armed forces.

We were shocked when Tim Palmer, the nicest boy in town, was the first in our community to be killed in action. Then his younger brother was called up, having to leave his grieving family. Every time I walked past the Palmer's house, my stomach churned as I noticed the blue star for their younger son hanging beside the gold star, which indicated that Jim was dead.

In 1942, we didn't talk much about the war in high school, but in mixed chorus we learned all the service-related songs and performed a medley in our spring concert. The Air Corps song was the one which made my blood surge as we sang, "Down we dive zooming to meet our thunder, at `em boys, give `er the gun. Give `er the gun!"

Mother handled the ration books, which were issued to each family member. We skimped on sugar, meat, shoes, gas and tires. But one commodity we didn't have to cut back on was liquor. Our family was opposed to drinking. Meatless Tuesdays were not a hardship because Mother was a fine cook and could always come up with some concoction. Macaroni and cheese with stewed tomatoes was the favorite. We didn't have a Victory Garden like some of our friends, but we did have asparagus growing in a corner of the yard. Mother would cut up the stalks and prepare them in a cream sauce served over toast to make them go a little farther. I hated it.

We saved our empty vegetable and soup cans for metal recycling by removing both the tops and bottoms which we would place inside the cylinder portion. We would flatten the cylinder by stepping on it to conserve space in the bin. We also saved balls of tin foil.

Daddy knew how to put half soles on my saddle shoes when they wore through to my bobby socks. We walked to all the places we could to save gas and tires. Even in the dark of night I walked alone to piano lessons or youth meetings at church with no fear of danger. It was a quiet town where people were nice to each other. I felt perfectly safe.

I became a student volunteer at the hospital. In the summer, a friend and I worked three afternoons a week in the lab, washing pipettes and cleaning equipment, trying to follow directions and endeavoring to be as efficient as we could under the stern eye of Miss Forsythe, the head technician. We were just kids playing grownup, but we knew we had to be responsible because Miss Forsythe was our mothers' friend, and we didn't want to risk a bad report.

Our small community hospital was short-staffed, so I continued to volunteer through the winter. I worked mornings before school, helping the nurses serve breakfasts. I didn't like getting up early and climbing the deserted, winding hill in the cold and pitch-black darkness to be on duty by seven o'clock.

Each floor had a small kitchen, about eight feet by six feet, where we cooked the bacon and made toast to accompany the oatmeal sent up from the main kitchen. One day, the nurse in charge was called away and I was on my own to cook the bacon. I didn't realize that it would burn quickly if left in its own fat on the hot plate. I almost ruined the entire batch, enveloping the small room in greasy smoke.

I never could understand their method of preparing tea for the ward. The instructions were to line up ten cups on the counter, fill them with hot water, and then, with one tea bag, go down the row with a quick dunk in each cup. As I delivered the trays, I wondered if those poor, sick people got a lift from their weak, lukewarm tea.

I was a bit of a menace on the floor. Some of my experiences convinced me that I definitely did not want to be a nurse. One morning I took a tray to a man in a private room who asked me to crank up his bed. I set the tray on the side table, not noticing that it hung over the bed about four inches. As I raised the bed, the mattress caught the edge of the tray and dumped everything.

Another morning I mistakenly gave breakfast to a man who was scheduled for surgery at ten o'clock, and he ate every bite. I never heard how the surgery went.

My worst task was being sent to feed a very sick man who had had his eyes removed—at least that is what I thought. As I spooned him his cereal, he lay there with empty, sunken sockets, not realizing that the person tending him was a frightened young girl prone to major mishaps.

By the time I was a high school senior, the war was escalating in Europe and in the Pacific. My boyfriend and some of the other bright boys in our class left midterm to enter the V-12, a Navy program on the college level. Johnny went to Villanova University. We wrote to each other every day. For Christmas, I proudly gave him a silver identification bracelet like those worn by many of the servicemen.

As I spooned him his cereal, he lay there with empty, sunken sockets, not realizing that the person tending him was a frightened young girl prone to major mishaps.

Only a few boys were around town by prom time, but I accepted a date with a nice fellow in our crowd who had gotten the okay from Johnny to invite me. I had a boring evening. It was memorable only because I could show off the beautiful full-length formal Mother had made for me. It was apple green, which I thought complemented my red hair.

I resisted making college plans. In fact, I thought I wanted to work for the FBI. A recruiter had come to school with an enticing message which sounded like a great chance for me to move away from my strict but loving home and do something important on my own. I even had my fingerprints taken. My parents were cool to the idea, knowing that if I went to Washington I would probably be a little fish in the typing pool. I couldn't even type. Visions of a grand opportunity were soon squelched. My parents sent me to summer school where I did learn to type and I was accepted at Wilson College, a women's school about four hours away in Pennsylvania.

In the fall of 1944, my brother was with the Air Force in Germany, my sister was living in her own apartment in

Pittsburgh, and I packed for college. I had to take my ration book and turn it in on arrival. Because travel was curtailed due to gas rationing, I had never seen the campus nor had I even met anyone from Wilson College. I left home that September day with a new acquaintance, another freshman from a nearby town.

Her father drove their Dodge sedan with all the suitcases, bags, and boxes we could manage to squeeze inside. Daddy shipped the rest of my things in an old steamer trunk. Our route directed us to the rear entrance of campus, past the maintenance plant and laundry, so my first view of my home for the next four years was terribly disappointing. I was soon overawed, however, by the acres of beautifully manicured, central Pennsylvania landscape dotted with imposing buildings—library, dorms, science hall—all seeming to call out, "Study, learn, work and maybe you'll even have a good time."

Since young men were scarce, I wasn't expecting to find the dating scene very interesting, but I was rescued by my roommate. We had just met when I learned she lived in a Philadelphia suburb. I immediately planned a weekend at her home near Villanova. It was wonderful. I had two days with Johnny whom I hadn't seen since he was home in June.

Big trouble hit me a few months later when I learned that he had become attracted to a spoiled, snobby daughter of a rich, Philadelphia Main Line contractor, and I became the girl of his past. Although I never expected to smile again, and my survival was in question for a while, I met an interesting man (we called them our "men") stationed at an Army intelligence base in Maryland who was older and quite sophisticated. So there!

Mary's newspaper photo, 1948

My college years were disrupted very little by the war. The head of our chemistry department was on leave, and we later learned that she had worked on the Manhattan Project, perfecting the atom bomb. Our dean was also on leave, serving in the WAVES at Hunter College where she directed a training program. She was replaced by an elderly woman—old but wonderful—who kept telling us how they did things at Smith College, where she had previously been on the faculty. She pronounced "Smith" with a pompous, guttural enunciation. We enjoyed mimicking her and thought ourselves hilarious.

The war ended in Europe the spring of my freshman year. I was excited to receive a telegram from my brother saying that he was returning to the States on the U.S.S. Argentina and would stop to see me in Chambersburg, Pennsylvania, on his way home.

V-J Day—victory over Japan—occurred the next August. That fall, Wilson accepted thirty returned veterans as day students. We called them our "coeds," and since most colleges were crowded with fellows studying on the GI Bill, our veterans stayed through the next year before transferring to other schools, which were then able to accept more men. The fact that we had no men on campus during the actual war years was a plus for us because we applied ourselves to our studies during the week and relaxed on weekends, sometimes entertaining visiting dates or going to nearby bases or other colleges where we could socialize.

It seems that my clearest memories of World War II revolve around men, or the absence of them. Perhaps my love affair with Van Johnson in *Thirty Seconds Over Tokyo* or Robert Walker in *The Clock* helped to create my mind set.

The most important part of my young life did not take place until after the hostilities ended. A young veteran named Bill at Gettysburg College, thirty miles over the mountains from my college, had chosen the school because his father and uncle were alumni, and it was a good school where he could pursue a business major. He had sustained serious injuries in the battle of St. Lo, France, and had recently been released from Ashford General Hospital in West Virginia, which specialized in orthopedic injuries.

Bill singing for returning GIs

In the spring of 1948, Bill noticed my picture in the newspaper. He liked what he saw and inquired about me from one of Wilson's former coeds, now a fellow student at Gettysburg. When he was told I was a redhead, he replied, "That's the cherry on the sundae." He was attracted to redheads and had visions of Maureen O'Hara. The short version of this episode is that a blind date was arranged, and after a few false starts, we began seeing each other. When he called me on the phone, he sounded like Nelson Eddy.

The distance between our two colleges was not a problem because he drove a brand new Oldsmobile. I thought he must be rich, but I learned that the government had given him the car upon his discharge. His injuries included permanent damage to his left leg, and Oldsmobile was the only make of car with automatic transmission at that time.

Before and after the war, Ashford General Hospital was the luxurious Greenbrier Hotel in White Sulphur Springs, West Virginia. Bill wanted to take me there for our honeymoon, but his friend, the manager, warned him that it would be much too expensive. We finally did spend a vacation there twenty-five years later.

Among Bill's appealing attributes was a heavenly singing voice, and in between his numerous operations at Ashford, he occasionally sang with visiting bands that performed for returning GIs. During our courtship, he would sing to me a song that became special for us both called, "I Could Make You Care." He did make me care, and we were married for forty-seven years.

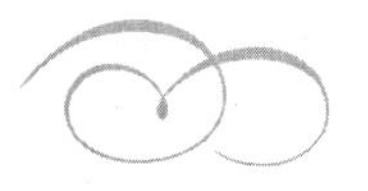

Annabelle Shober Saylor

Annabelle and her husband live in Harrisburg, Pennsylvania, with their three children and families living nearby. A retired teacher, Annabelle volunteers at a nursing home and at her church.

The same feelings come back to me today—how much it felt like a personal war! Almost every family had someone in the service. The war came right into our homes—not on television—but in some kind of war effort. Even though we lived in the country where we didn't even bother with blackouts, it was just as much our war, too.

At our home we didn't feel the food problem much because my father had a butcher shop. He had started out with an egg route, delivering eggs in a truck and then expanding to chickens and meat. He then became a successful butcher, W.L.Shober. He continued the delivery route and gradually added market stands in three large farmers markets in Reading, Pennsylvania. He employed about ten people at the peak of his business.

My older brother worked with him for awhile but then accepted a job in Delaware County working for a butcher. My other brother worked for our father until he could find a job that paid more money. Then he was drafted. My sister married and had a child, so she couldn't help in the business. I went along to market, but was quite young and not much of a salesperson. During the summer months, when I was fourteen to sixteen years old, I cooked a noon meal for the employees.

We had a smokehouse where we smoked our own hams, sausage, bologna and, once in awhile, turkeys. We killed our own steers, pigs, lambs, calves, chickens and turkeys.

We grew and canned fruits and vegetables. I remember the "war cake" my mother often used to make—no butter, no eggs. It had raisins in it. It was also called "poor man's cake," or "depression cake." Butter was rare and we used oleo that looked like lard and had to be colored with a coloring agent. It didn't taste good.

RECIPE FOR WAR CAKE

1 cup brown sugar
1 cup water
1/3 cup lard
1 cup seedless raisins
1 tsp. Salt
1 tsp. Cinnamon
1/2 tsp. Cloves (ground)
2 tsp. Cocoa
Mix and boil 3 minutes.
When cold add 1 tsp. baking soda dissolved in water, 2 cups flour, 1 tsp. baking powder.
Bake 350 degrees in 8x8-inch baking dish or pan, about 60 minutes.

We didn't suffer much from the gasoline shortage because we had our own gas tank, although the quantity was somewhat limited. Besides the trucks for the business, my dad owned a school bus and drove kids to two high schools. We lived under a mile from the school so I had to walk. Sometimes when my parents were away, I would let friends have a few gallons of gas, although not many teenagers had cars.

Our high school was on the main road between Lancaster and Reading where convoys of military vehicles would go by and sometimes even stop a bit. The trucks were loaded with soldiers—probably from Indiantown Gap—and the

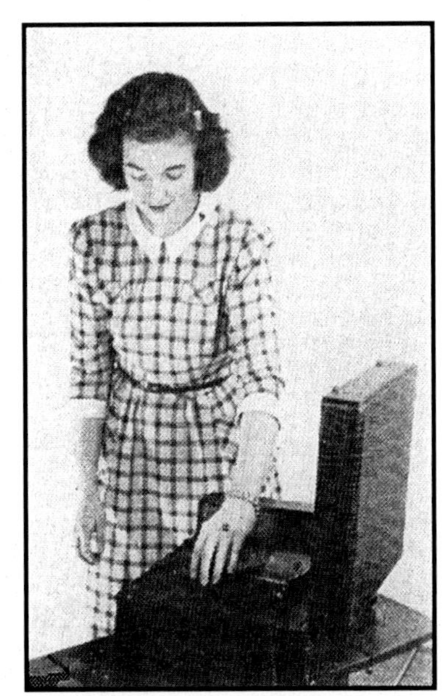

Annabelle operating record player at high school, 1944

boys would throw us their names and addresses. We often received pictures and would fantasize about the boys. I wrote to two of them but I don't recall any continuing connections.

We had a knitting club after school to make scarves, mittens, and socks for the servicemen. I had never knitted before and was glad to have the Home Economics teacher show me how. We also knitted squares for blankets. Most of our finished products were sent to the servicemen through the Red Cross, but some of the girls sent knitted items to the fellows who had thrown their addresses from the trucks.

Our Sunday School class helped in the door-to-door collection of aluminum foil (mostly from cigarettes packages and chewing gum wrappers), hardened cooking fat, and string, all to be used in the war. I think we also collected rubber.

The day after Pearl Harbor, we had an assembly and listened to President Roosevelt's "Day of Infamy" speech. Most of the girls were crying. To add to the trauma, our math teacher, John Hayes, stood up and said he was enlisting. He was so-o-o handsome, and the girls were crazy about him. It was so dramatic. Later, our young thirty-five year old principal was drafted.

Popular math teacher John Hayes

Our school was very small, but I remember three boys who enlisted. I wrote to one from our class and dated him for awhile when he returned. Two girls who graduated from high school the year before I did enrolled in nursing school. They were promised that they would have their schooling paid if they pre-enlisted, and would be made lieutenants upon graduation. They completed their training and worked in military hospitals. One went to the European Theater. Do you remember when the war zones were called "theaters?"

I began working in a parachute plant in my junior year in high school when I was only fifteen, and continued through the summer and into my senior year.

When my brother Roy was drafted, he was about twenty-four years old with two small children. He went to basic training in Alabama and was chosen for Officers' Candidate School (OCS). He concluded that his stay in the service would have been longer had he gone to OCS, so he declined. He was sent to Europe, was in France and then sent to Germany to help end the war in Europe. He came home soon after the victory in Europe and played on a touring camp basketball team. While he was away in the service, his wife and two children lived in an upstairs apartment in Denver, Pennsylvania. Roy said the song "Sentimental Journey" kept him going while he was away from his family.

I knew one watch tower observer. She was a bird watcher and already had binoculars. The towers were usually in wooded areas, so they weren't easily observed, but they were high enough so watchers could scan the skies. Many of us learned to recognize the various planes.

I began working in a parachute plant in my junior year in high school when I was only fifteen, and continued through the summer and into my senior year. The plant was very large and had previously housed a shoe factory. In some areas of the building, many machines were set up and women sat sewing the silk parachutes all day. Where I worked, there were long tables, about twenty feet long where the red silk parachutes were laid out. The parachutes had white cotton tape over the seams and were fastened by loops at the closed end. I stood at the other end with the cords that led from each seam. I would lay out one panel of the chute flat on the long table, then go up and down minutely examining the seams and the spaces between the seams, while at the same time, snipping off threads. When I finished one panel, I would turn over another panel. If I found a flaw, I pinned a yellow piece of cloth to the spot and the parachute would not be folded. The plant made only supply chutes, not people chutes. Almost all the factory employees were women. The bosses were men.

Music was important

Women vocalists on the radio meant a great deal to the people at home and to the servicemen. Songs were important. I remember Gracie Fields. She was sort of a comedienne as well as a singer and she sang cheerful songs. Vera Lynn, on the other hand, sang sad goodbye songs like "I'll be Seeing You," "White Cliffs of Dover," "We'll Meet Again—Don't Know Where, Don't Know When." And, of course, Kate Smith sang "God Bless America" every day at noon.

We all knew we were at war. We didn't need nightly television broadcasts to remind us.

Kathleen McCullough Akey

Following graduation from Ursinus College, Kathy studied at Northeastern University and Fairfield University. After twenty-eight years of teaching English in New Hampshire and Connecticut, she retired to her home in Trenton, New Jersey.

December 7, 1941. I was thirteen years old, holding the hand of my brother, who was twenty-five, as we joined friends and neighbors on our street, all of whom had gathered to discuss with fear and awe the catastrophic attack by the Japanese on Pearl Harbor. People spoke almost in whispers. As my brother Milt and I wandered from group to group, we heard many people say, "This means war." My brother looked down at me from his six foot two inches of height and said, "This is a day that both you and I will always remember because it will change our country's history forever." Indeed, it did.

My brother joined the Navy and, because of his skills as a welder and mechanic, was assigned to the Seabees and served in the Pacific. The men of the Seabees were experienced and talented carpenters, mechanics, engineers, and construction workers. They built airfields on the Pacific Islands with the motto, "The difficult we do today; the impossible tomorrow." These airfields were essential to move men and equipment to the islands for the war against the well-entrenched Japanese. My brother was awarded a certificate of distinction for his work on the flamethrower, which was used to attack the Japanese who were hidden in caves on the various islands. Mail from him was always a highlight for my family, but few details of his life in the service were forthcoming. Mail was carefully censored for security reasons, so we became accustomed to the receipt of letters with large portions obliterated by the heavy dark lines of the censor.

My brother was awarded a certificate of distinction for his work on the flamethrower

Kathy's brother Milt

In the meantime, life at home went on at a fairly normal pace. My parents, along with many of our neighbors, planted a Victory Garden of tomatoes, carrots, beans, etc. We adjusted to the demands of ration stamps, which were used for shortages such as flour, sugar, shoes, and gasoline. Very few of our neighbors had cars, since gasoline was in short supply. We children liked to sit on our porches and identify the cars as they drove by, with their distinctive hood logos. Chevrolet, Ford, and Buick were chief among them.

The seeming normalcy of our lives in the neighborhood was shattered when my mother came home from her job as a telephone operator to announce somberly that Eddie Slovak, the son of a neighbor, had been killed in the war. His family had placed a gold star in their window, signaling to all who walked past that a mother had lost her soldier son. I was a very happy child, secure with family and friends both at home and at school, but I could never walk by that house without a feeling of dread and wonder. We kids had played on the street with Eddie, and to think of him as dead was fearful. If it could happen to Eddie, it could happen to my beloved brother, Milt.

I was a freshman in high school in 1941. With the war concluding in 1945, my experience was seen not only through my life at home but also at school. We had to accept that some of our favorite male teachers would leave for the armed forces. In my senior year, many of the boys in our class also left for military service. During the four years of the war, we students sold Savings Bonds, knitted socks and mittens for the Red Cross, wrote letters to servicemen we knew, and tried to learn the geography of the war from our teachers who had us follow maps of the battles in Europe and in the Pacific.

I was an ardent reader of the reports from the war written by the famous correspondent Ernie Pyle. Pyle had the love and respect of the men among whom he served, since his interest in them was always the personal. He did not dwell on battle statistics but on the reactions and emotions of the men who participated. He always portrayed them as heroic, courageous, and admirable. This gave readers like me hope that we would prevail over our enemies. Sadly, Ernie Pyle was killed by enemy fire on the island of Ie Shima, off the coast of Okinawa, in April of 1945, shortly before the end of the war.

My sister, who was three years older than I, had the envious opportunity of attending dances at Fort Dix with servicemen who were often stationed there just before being sent overseas. She belonged to a group called the Rainbow Girls, whose sponsors would provide buses to take the girls to Fort Dix for an evening of dancing. Miriam, then seventeen, would prepare for the dance all afternoon by donning a lovely evening gown, using makeup much more lavishly than permitted under normal circumstances, and fixing her hair in a special style, the "up-sweep."

Young men going overseas often proposed marriage on the spot, an indication of their insecurities about not returning home.

I was envious at the fun she would have and disgruntled by being told I was too young to go. But I always waited up for her report of the evening. She often declared with a laugh that she had had two proposals of marriage that night. It seems that young men going overseas often proposed marriage on the spot, perhaps an indication of their insecurities about not returning home and wanting to live life fully before they left for the unknown.

In the summers of 1944 and 1945, I worked the four-to-twelve shift at Western Union, taking telegrams over the phone. Many of the messages were to and from service personnel, often from anxious wives who had not heard from their spouses for some time. One evening a young soldier stood at the front desk for at least two hours, asking every twenty minutes or so if his message had come through with the money he had requested from family or friends. Finally, I took pity on him and advanced him ten dollars. He assured me that he would mail the loan to me very soon but, of course, that promise was never fulfilled.

My first job, soon after obtaining working papers at age sixteen, was in sales at our local five and dime. Every day a young woman, perhaps nineteen, would visit us at the store and wander the aisles commenting upon the merchandise but rarely buying anything except a bit of candy. Soon she began to tell us about herself. Her husband was stationed at Fort Dix and she had only a little room nearby. She knew no one and saw her husband infrequently. It was, upon reflection, a very sad life, and I often wonder what happened to this vivacious and attractive young woman. She was representative of the many lonely young women who courageously waited for their loved ones to return from the war.

In April of 1945 we learned of the death of our beloved president, Franklin D. Roosevelt. It was a terrible irony. He had led us so valiantly through the war and had met his death just as the war was concluding. I was chosen by the faculty of my high school to give the tribute to our President in the assembly. I was very proud of that moment and proud of the program of remembrance, filled with music and memorable tributes created by our faculty.

In the fall I was off to Ursinus College where, in my freshman year, we young women lived in a men's dormitory recently vacated by the V-12 program, devised to train young men to be naval officers. Our freshman year was peaceful and happy, altered greatly in 1946 when our returning servicemen took advantage of the GI Bill by enrolling in colleges across the country. We women had to vacate Brodbeck, a men's dorm, so that these veterans could be accommodated. We were scattered to homes throughout the small town of Collegeville, Pennsylvania. My roommate and I were assigned to a house that had been a florist shop. The property was in great need of repair when we thirteen female students were moved into it, with only one standard bathroom.

Kathy in 1945

The men made quite a difference in the culture of the campus. At first we were shocked and dismayed at some of the servicemen who were disfigured by severe burns. A number of them were bused over to Ursinus every day from Valley Forge General Hospital. They came on crutches, with heads and arms bandaged, and many with the haunted eyes of young men who had seen and experienced the horrors of war.

At first we were shocked and dismayed at some of the servicemen who were disfigured by severe burns.

We were made fully aware of our naiveté and immaturity by the dominant positions taken by the men. They were quite outspoken in their viewpoints in our classes and came to dominate leadership positions in almost all campus activities. But a clear indication of our love and acceptance of these men is the fact that many romances led to marriages of classmates.

Upon our graduation from college in 1949, we returned home to find that housing was very difficult to obtain for newly married couples, and jobs were tilted toward the hiring of returning servicemen. This was to be expected, but women who had filled factory jobs and teaching jobs during the absence of the men now found it difficult to find employment, and a bias existed toward many women who did continue to work.

The economy had picked up dramatically as demands for cars and household goods escalated. My brother returned safely from his tour of duty with the Seabees, and found a job immediately as a welder with the U. S. Aircraft Company of Trenton, New Jersey.

Servicemen were held in high esteem. Americans were proud of our victories, and the United States was respected all around the globe. It was a good time to be alive and to be an American.

Margaret Hewitt George

Peggy served on her local school board and in the Pennsylvania House of Representatives. Aside from enjoying family and friends, she has done extensive genealogical research.

My first inkling that all was not well in the world beyond my immediate environs—Chester, Pennsylvania—came in the mid-1930s. Among the many children living in the section of the city known as Sun Hill was my playmate, Martin Schultz. Putey was his nickname. He is the only person I remember ever having had the mumps, and Putey's mumps kept him from attending my birthday party. Putey was from Germany, but he and his parents spoke English. He walked to Martin Elementary School past PMC (then Pennsylvania Military College, now Widener University) with the neighborhood gang.

One day in May, Putey didn't go to school. The rest of us children thought he was just sick and we didn't think too much about it. But when we arrived home, the neighborhood mothers were huddled together discussing something very important. The Schultz house was empty! The family had moved out in the middle of the night, without telling a soul. Putey's father had worked at the Sun Shipyard and that's when I heard the word "spy" and that's when I learned "we" didn't like Germans. I was upset. I liked Putey and I would miss him. And maybe his father wasn't a spy after all.

I heard the word "spy" and that's when I learned "we" didn't like Germans.

The years passed and war came—not only with Germany, but also with Japan. My brother Charles had been in the Reserve Officers Training Corps (ROTC) at Drexel College and went immediately into the service upon graduation. He was a meteorologist on the Aleutian Islands. My brother George tried twice to enlist in the Navy as a chaplain's assistant, but since he was a ministerial student at Dickinson College, he was turned down. Instead, since the need for ordained clergy to serve as chaplains was great, he was encouraged to minister to a small congregation while continuing his studies. He tells of the embarrassment he and a fellow ministerial student felt when they were the object of much ridicule as they rode home from college in a train filled with servicemen. Most able-bodied young men were in the service. To avoid further mocking comments, George and his friend stood in the little section between cars.

When I was sixteen, I went to work at Westinghouse Electric Company in Lester, Pennsylvania, during the summer months. The company had converted to making products for the war effort.

I remember my first day. We began work at 8:00 a.m. and worked until 5:00 p.m., with two fifteen minute breaks and a half-hour break for lunch. On my morning break, I saw all these women in a lounge outside the bathroom area, sitting around talking loudly and smoking. I felt awkward and very much out of place. I headed back to the security of my office as quickly as possible.

I was the youngest person in the Purchasing Department and I loved my job. I worked long hours, six days a week. On my first day I was directed to file some purchase orders. I asked if I should put them in the drawers after I had sorted them, or did someone want to check my work up to that point. "No, just file," I was told. So I did, and I'm sure my filing was at least 99% accurate.

[A side note here. Six years later, as a college graduate, I went to work in a university library. When asked to file 3x5 index cards, my boss told me to tilt the card so she could check my work. At Westinghouse, we were all so busy pumping out purchase orders, it was assumed we would do our work right the first time.]

One of our major tasks was to make sure the purchase orders were correct. Some of them were quite long—four, five, or six pages—consisting of many items. After the typists prepared the purchase orders, two other office workers would use rulers, sliding down each item to check the correctness. One person would read from the hand-written order prepared by a salesman or a phone clerk, the other would check for accuracy on the order to be sent to the vendor.

My work at Westinghouse was satisfying. I really didn't think I was helping the war effort, although I certainly was. I thought I was just making money to go to college. As for the long hours, many other people were working six days a week and some were working seven days. It was all part of the war effort.

Peggy's father's Victory Garden

A friend of my parents was the night superintendent at Sun Ship, and he worked seven nights a week. I was allowed to skip school the day his wife christened a war ship. I can still see her whacking the ship with a bottle of champagne.

My mother knit long white bandages and several khaki sweaters, and my father tended his Victory Garden of tomatoes, beans, lettuce, and other produce while working at the Sun Oil Company in Philadelphia. It was necessary for housewives to carefully plan meals, given the shortage of various important ingredients—sugar, butter, meats and other products. I recall being sent to the store once with my ration stamps in hand, only to realize I had forgotten to take money.

Gasoline rationing dramatically changed our every-other Sunday visits to my grandparents in Delaware. Before the war, the trip was a leisurely Sunday afternoon outing by car, first to visit my maternal grandfather in Wilmington and then to New Castle to visit my paternal grandmother. Once gasoline rationing went into effect, the visits were reduced to once a month by bus and train to Wilmington, then another bus to New Castle. And back home again via the same transportation.

I graduated from high school just prior to the end of the war. My parents had to scrape to send my brothers to college and were not sold on the idea of my going to college. But with guidance from my high school principal, my work in the summers, and with generous financial help from Ursinus College, I set off for Collegeville, Pennsylvania, in the fall of 1945. Part of the financial aid was in the form of self-help work. My job was cleaning the rooms on my dorm floor. If I had received a grade for my job performance, I'm afraid I would

The cleaning woman and her mop

have failed. After my freshman year, I became a waitress and then a library assistant, for which I was much better suited.

In college, we were reminded on a daily basis of the cost of war. Wounded servicemen stationed at the Valley Forge General Hospital in Phoenixville were bused to Ursinus each day. They came with entire faces bandaged from burns. I recall my philosophy professor acknowledging in class how humble he felt in their presence while attempting to lead the class in discussions on the meaning and nature of life. He recognized how trite some of the material must seem to these men who had witnessed death on many occasions. Nevertheless, we saw the men recover, become integrated into the college scene, and marry some of our classmates.

Aside from these wounded soldiers, a large influx of veterans swarmed onto college and university campuses, making use of the GI Bill. Among those who came to Ursinus was a good-looking guy named Glenn George, my husband for fifty-four years.

Among those who came to Ursinus was a good-looking guy named Glenn George, my husband for fifty-four years.

When the war was over, the country was anxious to return to normalcy, whatever normalcy was. We had been little children during the Depression. As elementary school students, we were aware of the invasion of many European countries by Adolf Hitler, and in high school we had seen our brothers, classmates, and teachers go off to war. Now, with the war ended and our servicemen and women returning home, we looked forward to the years ahead with much joy and great optimism.

Shurley Knaefler Whittaker Josephson

Shurley graduated from North Wales High School and Ursinus College in Pennsylvania. She has one daughter, two sons and five grandchildren. Shurley participates in church and other volunteer activities, and enjoys travel, antiques, and bridge.

I was raised in North Wales, Pennsylvania, where my father was Assistant Postmaster for many years and my mother was active in church and civic club activities. I had no brothers or sisters, so I was particularly glad for opportunities to be with my cousins.

For a week each summer, I visited with my aunt and cousins in Surf City, New Jersey. At that time, homes right on the beach were unusual, so we felt quite lucky that my aunt and uncle had one. It was such fun to walk out the front door, go over a dune, and be right at the ocean. There were no lifeguards, just a long stretch of beach with waves sparkling in the sun. During the war years, we had to draw the black shades at night so no light would shine outside.

Shurley in 1943

Each night soldiers from a nearby Army post patrolled the beach, always in pairs. My aunt had great compassion for these lonely soldiers, as she called them, and would make sandwiches and goodies that we would take to them as they walked. What excitement! My older cousin, Patsy, an attractive blonde, was the object of affection from a dirigible pilot. When he would fly low over the water, he would call out on the megaphone to her as she walked on the beach, "See you tomorrow night at eight." I was duly impressed.

My dad was an air raid warden and would go at night to the roof of the high school. There were always two volunteers who stayed together.

Several months after World War II began, my dad, who was forty-six years old at the time and had served in France during World War I, applied for a commission in the Army Specialist Corps. To advance his cause, he secured letters of recommendation from many acquaintances and former Army friends. But after a period of some months, he received a letter from the War Department advising him that, "at the present time the requirements of the Army for the direct appointment of commissioned officers have been met." It must have been quite a blow to this very patriotic man.

I have often wondered how my mother felt about my dad's attempt to enlist since it would have affected her life greatly. My father had planned for Mother and me to move to a smaller place that was being vacated while he would rent our home to someone else until his re-

The boys' shop teacher worked the night shift at Philadelphia Electric and taught during the day. The English teacher operated a granite memorial business.

turn. Of course, as it turned out, none of these arrangements had to be carried out.

My dad was an air raid warden and would go at night to the roof of the high school. There were always two volunteers who stayed together. Many people volunteered with civil defense projects. When the siren sounded, we had to pull down the black window shades and stay inside. After a half-hour or so, the all-clear siren would sound and we could resume normal activities.

Since some of our male teachers had enlisted and because most college graduates were going immediately into the service, a teacher shortage existed. Some of the people hired to teach had few qualifications, but many were skilled in their fields. The boys' shop teacher worked the night shift at Philadelphia Electric and taught during the day. The English teacher operated a granite memorial business in the area.

SKF, a ball bearing plant nearby, produced goods for the war effort. A number of qualified students were employed there during after-school hours. One of my friends worked the four-to-seven shift two days a week and all day Saturday. I wanted to work there, too, but my parents wouldn't let me.

I played hockey and basketball in high school. During the war years, busing to and from games was discontinued, making it necessary for parents and teachers to drive us. One day when sufficient drivers were unavailable, the coach asked me to drive. I told her she would have to ask my father. She

Sun-Telegraph

EXTRA

President Truman Announces:

WAR OVER

McArthur to Rule Japan

did, and he said it was all right. I had taken my driver's test the day I was sixteen. Because my mother did not drive, my father was eager for me to have my license, thus freeing him up from driving us to our various activities.

On several occasions, some of us high school girls went to Valley Forge General Hospital to help entertain wounded servicemen. Sometimes we read to them, played games with them, and put on skits.

Our graduating class consisted of twenty-eight students, five of whom enlisted before June. In April, our class went by train to New York, staying at the New Yorker Hotel for one night. Such fun it was to visit the Statue of Liberty, attend a show at Radio City Music Hall and to stand at the top of the Empire State Building. We kept in touch with the graduating servicemen through a school-sponsored mimeographed mailing, which included copies of their letters to us.

V-J Day in August of 1945! What a long-awaited and joyful time it was. Two of my cousins, one in the Navy and the other in the Army, returned to their families. A friend who had been captured in the Battle of the Bulge and had been a Ger-

Shurley's father's flag from World War I

man prisoner of war for three months returned safely to his family in Andover, Massachusetts. Soon thereafter, I left for my freshman year at Ursinus College in Collegeville, Pennsylvania.

For many years, our family picnics were highlighted by the presence of my father's huge American flag from World War I. It was approximately twenty by ten feet, hung vertically on a line running from our house to a large tree by the street. The flag was a reminder of the sacrifices made by many to ensure our country's freedom.

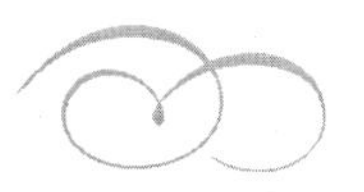

Jeanne Miller Oglesby

Jeanne, a lifelong resident of Phoenixville, Pennsylvania, is a retired cost accountant. She has six grandchildren and two great-grandchildren. Jeanne enjoys travel, gardening, reading, and volunteering activities.

When I think of World War II, most of my memories are of my high school days. I was a sophomore at Phoenixville High School in Chester County, Pennsylvania, attending school from twelve noon until 4:30 p.m. We were on half-day sessions—the juniors and seniors attending from 8:00 a.m. until 12:30 p.m. and sophomores reporting to school at noon.

Having the morning free gave me the opportunity to answer the call for help at the nearby Kimberton Farms, a collection of seven farms each with a different purpose dedicated to organic or regenerative farming at a time when the trend was toward increased use of chemicals. My two girlfriends and I worked mostly at the main farm where we did a variety of tasks. We cared for a large herb garden—weeding and cultivating the herbs, which we were told were being grown for medicinal purposes. We spent a whole day cutting up potatoes and making sure each piece had an eye so they could be planted. We also burned caterpillar tents in trees, cut down weeds using a scythe, and periodically turned compost piles. Our pay was thirty-five cents an hour.

Jeanne in 1945

Because of gas rationing, girls' interscholastic sports were eliminated during my high school years.

Many students had jobs while attending school. It is reported that seventy-three students of our 125-member 1945 graduating class were employed, many of them in area defense industries including Jacob Aircraft Company, B. F. Goodrich Company, Phoenix Iron and Steel Company, and Synthane Corporation. Additionally, by the time we graduated, fourteen of our classmates and five of our teachers had entered the service. A number of teachers were also employed in local defense industries.

Because of gas rationing, girls' interscholastic sports were eliminated during my high school years. This was a disappointment since I had been selected for the basketball team.

Our high school band, of which I was a member, received a "Music War Council of America's Distinguished Service" citation for its musical contribution to the war effort. These included playing at the railroad station for selectees (draftees) as they boarded the train, giving concerts for patients at Valley Forge General Hospital, participating in a Red Cross benefit show, "Something for the Boys," and various performances related to the war effort.

My father owned and operated a retail bakery in Phoenixville. The war had a huge effect on his business, which depended very much on eggs, butter and sugar, all of which were rationed.

He was also an air raid warden and firewatcher. In 1939, the Phoenix Iron and Steel Corporation installed an air raid whistle at its plant, which could be heard for miles. When that whistle blew, my father had to go out onto the third floor roof (we lived above the bakery) to be on guard for fires and other unusual circumstances. What an eerie feeling it was when the whole town was plunged into darkness except for the red glow lighting up the sky from the open hearth furnace at the iron works—a prime target for the enemy.

The opening of Valley Forge General Hospital on Washington's birthday in February of 1943 impacted Phoenixville in many ways. Located just outside the borough limits in Charlestown Township, it specialized in treating wounded soldiers in need of plastic surgery, eye surgery, and rehabilitation due to blindness. These soldiers became a familiar sight on the local streets and a USO was established downtown where local citizens volunteered as hostesses, dance partners, entertainers, etc. They also volunteered in the wards as visitors doing whatever they could to serve as a substitute family for the wounded. More than one soldier decided to remain in Phoenixville after discharge and marry a local gal.

Jeanne and her brother Forrest

The hospital and Phoenixville gained fame by the release of the movie, "Bright Victory," based on a book telling the story of a blinded soldier and his rehabilitation. The movie depicted what was a very common sight for us—a sighted soldier teaching a blinded soldier how to navigate his way by tapping his cane from side to side, and showing him how and when to cross a street.

Phoenixville had an active Red Cross branch providing many services to families and to soldiers. Since there were no motels in town and only a few hotel rooms available, members of the community opened their homes for visitors requiring short stays. Mother rolled bandages one night a week at the downtown headquarters.

My brother, Forrest Miller, served with the 5th Air Force in the South Pacific as they made their way from island to island, becoming one of the first units to be sent to occupy Japan after its surrender. He had been an engineering student at Drexel University enrolled in the ROTC. These students were initially deferred, but in the spring of 1943, he was called up. In December of 1945, he sailed from Yokohoma, Japan, arriving home mid-January of 1946.

Of my seven male cousins, six of them served in various branches of the service. The seventh cousin, a medical student at Jefferson University Hospital, was deferred from active duty. With the shortage of doctors he was overworked as an intern, and by the time he was treating tuberculosis patients on his last rotation, he was so physically spent that he, too, contracted the disease.

Ford Oglesby, who became my husband in 1960, served in the "Big Red One," the Army's 1st Infantry Division in France, Belgium, and Germany. Later he was assigned to headquarters as a staff writer. Ford was one of the oldest individuals called up in 1944. He was twenty-eight years old and had previously been deferred because of age and because he

We were listening to Lowell Thomas this evening and immediately after he said, "So long until tomorrow," the newsrooms in Washington gave the news that the war had ended.

was married with a young child. He was discharged in January, 1946 after having been brought home on an emergency leave to see his mother who was gravely ill. Unfortunately, she died before he arrived.

In the summer of 1945, following my graduation from high school, several friends and I took summer jobs as waitresses at the Hotel Delaware in Ocean City, New Jersey. We had to turn over our ration books to the hotel temporarily because we were given room and board as part of the deal. But the hotel really took advantage of us waitresses. Meat was a rationed item and the hotel had our meat ration stamps. We were served meat only several times all summer! I spent lots of tip money buying hamburgers on the boardwalk.

After serving dinner the evening of V-J Day in August, 1945, we waitresses caught a trolley to Atlantic City where we knew the celebration would be more exciting. Aside from being a livelier town, the government had taken over some of Atlantic City's large hotels such as the Chalfonte-Haddon Hall to provide R&R for servicemen, particularly the wounded. That night the boardwalk was alive with excitement and noise. Bells were ringing, servicemen were throwing crutches into the air, and people were grabbing strangers to dance with. Joy was everywhere. We were too young to be part of the bar scene, so I cannot report on that, and unfortunately, we could only stay a short time as we had to catch the last trolley back to Ocean City.

Meanwhile, Mother wrote a letter to my brother and me at 10:45 the evening of V-J Day, telling us about the celebration in Phoenixville. Here is an edited version:

The wonderful time is here! We were listening to Lowell Thomas this evening and immediately after he said, "So long until tomorrow," the newsrooms in Washington gave the news that the war had ended. Five minutes later the Iron Company whistle began blowing and did not let up for one half hour! The fire sirens started blowing, cars honked their horns, and every kind of noisemaker was used, from sleigh bells to dinner bells.

Kids tied cans to their bicycles and the American Legion, which had been trying to revive the Drum Corp, made a brave impromptu attempt. Fire engines came out in full force with bells clanging and sirens blowing. Cars streamed in from the surrounding countryside, decked with banners and overflowing with kids. Paper littered the streets.

Everyone had a wonderful time. Churches were open for worship, and while most of us gave immediate thanks upon hearing the news, I doubt if very many attended church. This was one time everyone had the urge to demonstrate. Dad mixed us a ginger ale highball and we went out to enjoy the fun. The manager of the USO was handing out cigars to the soldiers, and the old firehouse bell rang for fifteen minutes, the first time they had used the bell since they retired the horses. It was a wonderful evening!

The war was finally over, and in the fall of 1945, I began my freshman year at Ursinus College, Collegeville, Pennsylvania. During the second semester, veterans, including my brother, began attending Ursinus under the benefits of the GI Bill in hopes of resuming their lives, which had been severely disrupted by war.

MAKE SURE THEY'RE SUNK–
BRING IN YOUR JUNK!
THE JUNK ON YOUR FARM
DEPOSIT SCRAP HERE
Save waste fats for explosives
TAKE THEM TO YOUR MEAT DEALER
Fuel Fights!
SAVE YOUR SHARE
1 Keep temperature at 65° F. during day - lower at night.
2 Don't heat unused rooms.
3 Keep windows closed.
4 Draw window shades at night.
5 Shut off heat when weather permits.
6 Keep heating plant in top condition.
7 Use less hot water.
Saving fuel also saves manpower, material, equipment
CONSERVE COAL, OIL, GAS... FOR WAR

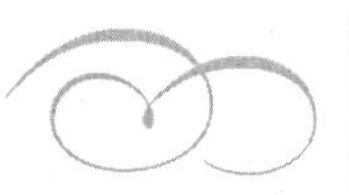

Barbara Yerkes Mitchell

Barbara and her husband live in Levittown, Pennsylvania, and Fort Myers, Florida. They have a daughter, son, and six grandchildren. Barbara taught in Bristol, Pennsylvania, and for many years officiated hockey and basketball.

I grew up on a 235-acre farm in the Village of Buckingham in Bucks County, Pennsylvania. Food was never a problem for us, not even during the war years. My dad grew a large vegetable garden, which he was very proud of, and Mother canned shelves of vegetables and fruits from the produce grown on our farm. Freezing was not yet an option.

In the early forties, my dad was the largest grower of sweet corn in Pennsylvania. He came up with the idea of picking the corn at night, which was then delivered early in the morning to stores in the Philadelphia area. Thus, "First Day Corn" became a reality. Dad frequently shipped tractor-trailer loads of corn to an Army depot nearby. He always said that the government payment was prompt.

One spring, my dad made an agreement with another farmer to cut the asparagus on his farm. So my brothers and I cut asparagus for the season every morning before we went to school. Whenever extra help was needed for farm chores, I was tapped to drive trucks for loading bales of hay and straw.

Farmers always need extra help with their harvest, but during the war years, the shortage of farm workers was a severe problem. In the fall, we went as a class from Buckingham High School to pick apples. The gasoline shortage didn't effect our farm operations at all. Farmers were the first to be supplied.

Farmers always need extra help with their harvest, but during the war years, the shortage of farm workers was a severe problem.

Barb and her father sorting corn

My mother volunteered to be an aircraft spotter. She would go to an air-raid shelter near Doylestown, Pennsylvania, and any plane that flew over the area was reported. This she did on a weekly basis. She also would send lunch out to the farm workers in the field when it was threshing time. These men went from farm to farm with their equipment. Later, my dad bought his own equipment. I was still in high school for much of the war. There were no buses for after-school activities and since the school was close to the farm, my brothers and I often had extra students come home with us for meals. Our family was active in the Grange, and we had many friends who met there for dinners and social times. All of us took piano lessons. At school we sang in choruses and played musical instruments.

We had a number of local boys from high school leave before graduation to go to basic training. My class at Buckingham High was to have twenty-one graduates, but on graduation night only fifteen seniors were present at the Grange Hall for the service. I wrote to several of the fellows and still have a letter from one marine who served in the South Pacific. Of course, all these letters were heavily censored before being sent on to me. I don't remember any women from Buckingham going into the service.

Being the oldest in the family, going away to college was a big experience. We didn't go home often, partly because of the gasoline shortage. Our children can't believe that I mailed my laundry home! We all did. Automatic washers and dryers had not yet come to college dorms. Fortunately, I made wonderful friends while at Ursinus College—and still get together with several of them for lunch regularly.

I am thankful for my farm family background and my family heritage.

Barb's brother Skip, her math teacher Maude Funk Large, Barb, her English and French teacher Betty Berger Porter, farm worker, and her brother John

FOOD IS A WEAPON
DON'T WASTE IT!
BUY WISELY - COOK CAREFULLY - EAT IT ALL
FOLLOW THE NATIONAL WARTIME NUTRITION PROGRAM
Grow Your Own
FRUITS AND VEGETABLES
Food Will Win the War and Write the Peace
Secretary, U.S. Department of Agriculture
Save
ALL YOU
RAISE
BUY UNITED STATES WAR BONDS AND STAMPS
INTERNATIONAL HARVESTER

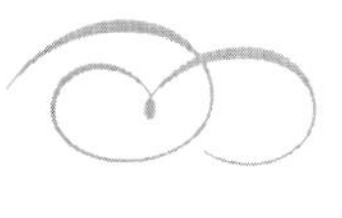

Elizabeth Gross Hendricks Miller

Liz has lived in Buckingham, Pennsylvania, for the past thirty years. Her extended family and her travels to unusual countries continue to build memories to treasure.

My father, Walter Gross, had a haberdashery business on Germantown Avenue in Philadelphia, Pennsylvania. He sold men's furnishings with the exception of shoes, suits and overcoats. Prior to the war, he and all the other businesses in the neighborhood were open every evening. Thereafter, in order to conserve electricity, they were open evenings only on weekends.

My family was of German descent, my father having arrived in Philadelphia as a boy of twelve. He and his father left behind in Germany my grandmother, my father's two sisters, and two brothers. My father began working immediately in a small bakery at Second and Brown Streets, which was a German community. His father, who was a trained wheelwright on the other side (back in Germany), had made wheels for the royal carriages in Romania. After two years in the United States, my father and grandfather had accumulated enough money to send for the remainder of the family.

Later my father went to work at the Stetson Hat Company where he learned the hat trade. He was able to save enough money to open his own store on Germantown Avenue near Erie Avenue. I have always been amazed how he learned English, even without any schooling.

My father retained his German interests and belonged to the German social/athletic club known as The Philadelphia Turngeminde, also known as the Turners. My father so loved gymnastics that he had a set of parallel bars installed behind his store where he practiced his handstands regularly.

My father didn't want people to perceive him as being a German sympathizer.

Starting at the age of five, I took gymnastic lessons twice a week at Turners until I was fourteen. I had always wanted to be a gym teacher but my father felt gymnastics was unladylike because I would develop large muscles. This early training was a large part of my life and I hated to give it up.

We always received the German newspaper, *Der Zeitung*, published in Philadelphia. It was available for store customers to browse through, but with the advent of the war,

Liz's father on his parallel bars behind his store

my father cancelled his subscription. He didn't want people to perceive him as being a German sympathizer. We did send food packages to relatives in Germany since the need was so great. My father would send me to the post office with the packages, which I remember were sent to Berlin.

I rode the trolley every day to Lankenau School for Girls in Germantown. Advertisements were posted along the body of the trolley, and one pictured a large close-up of a person with a finger pressed to the lips saying "Shhh, someone may be listening." People were cautioned not to reveal any information that might hinder the war effort.

Because of the many nurses serving in the war effort, a shortage existed on the home front. During my senior year of high school I was a Junior Nurses Aide at the Women's Medical College Hospital, walking about a mile to the hospital after school twice a week. My jobs were menial—mainly delivering mail and filling water pitchers. But one day a doctor requested help in the delivery room. I didn't go.

Liz in 1945

I recall some of the neighborhood women knitting mufflers for the soldiers, using wool supplied by the Red Cross. And we all saved rendered fat in coffee cans. This was used to make explosives.

My cousin was a career Navy man, serving in Japan during the occupation. We were, of course, anxious about him and always looked forward to his letters, even though portions of the letters were blacked out by the censors.

Before the war, my father bought a house in Ocean City, New Jersey, where my mother, my sister and I spent the summers. My father came down late Saturday night after closing the store and returned to Philadelphia Sunday evening. After retirement he was able to enjoy our summer home to a much greater degree. I had a summer job at Shrivers' at Ninth Street on the boardwalk, packing and wrapping saltwater taffy.

During the war, special precautions were taken along the Jersey shore to preclude the enemy from seeing our coastline. The light standards along the boardwalk were blackened on the ocean side and our window shades were black, so that no light at all could be seen.

We often saw convoys of ships offshore on their way to active duty. Their presence made the war even more real. Globs of oil and tar from the ships accumulated on the beach, leaving bathers with the problem of removing them from the soles of their feet, and even from their bathing suits. We found Crisco did the best job.

People who owned powerboats were encouraged to donate them to the Navy for patrolling the shore. In Atlantic

We often saw convoys of ships offshore on their way to active duty. Their presence made the war even more real.

City, some of the hotels were taken over by the military to be used for servicemen wounded in the war, and those who were able often sat on the upper porches. I recall a visit to Atlantic City and waving to these men.

Coupons for sugar, butter, shoes, etc., were issued for every member of the family. When I entered Ursinus College in the fall of 1945, just after the armistice was signed, food shortages were still rampant. Therefore, our food coupons had to be sent to the college along with our tuition.

Entertaining the servicemen at USOs, churches, and in private homes was encouraged. For the servicemen to have a home-cooked meal was considered a special treat. My sister, three years older than I, prevailed upon our parents to go through the necessary steps to invite two servicemen for dinner one night. My sister Dot's best friend from school would also attend. The plan was for Dot and her friend to meet the servicemen as they exited the subway station and then proceed to our home.

I made it my business to hurry along ahead of them and position myself behind the heavy metal grillwork where I had a close-up view of the meeting, which never happened. As the soldiers came up the subway steps onto the street, they pretended they didn't see Dot and her friend. And then I heard one of them say to the other, "The first one wasn't too bad, but when the second one came along, that was too much!"

They escaped! No company for dinner that night!

Marian Bacon Whitcomb

Mernie lives in Bristol, Connecticut, and has four children, fifteen grandchildren and three great-grandchildren. She is active in her church and is leader of the stroke group in which her husband was a member.

World War II occurred during my high school years. At that point in my life, I wasn't particularly interested in world affairs, but I certainly was aware of the war!

My brother was serving in the Navy and was commander of a LCI (Landing Craft Infantry) that participated in the D-Day invasion. He was not allowed to tell his whereabouts, but he wrote in a letter to Mother that he had visited Aunt Susie. Mother had a dear friend, Susie, living in England, so she knew my brother had been sent there.

We had quite a few boys in our high school class leave during our senior year to serve in the armed forces. Every so often, they would visit high school in their new uniforms, looking quite proud and enjoying the attention from the rest of us. We girls had their addresses and wrote to many of them. My high school boy friend enlisted in the Air Force as soon as we graduated, and my sister had a good friend whose brother was killed in the war. That really hit home. We could hardly believe it.

Mernie in 1945

I remember the horror we felt when Japan attacked Pearl Harbor on December 7, 1941. We huddled around the radio (there was no TV then) to get all the news we could. Our folks were really upset. We depended on the radio daily to keep abreast of what was going on, listening particularly to Edward R. Murrow broadcast from London.

We depended on the radio daily to keep abreast of what was going on, listening particularly to Edward R. Murrow broadcast from London.

My father was a mechanical engineer working at Westinghouse at the Lester plant, not far from our home in Prospect Park, Pennsylvania. The plant had geared up for the war effort. Mother volunteered at the Red Cross offices in Chester, Pennsylvania, where she assisted soldiers and their families in times of crisis, such as the death or serious illness of a family member here in the States. If possible, the soldiers would be brought home on temporary leave.

Supplies were scarce, and we had ration stamps for coffee, sugar, butter, gas, shoes and other items. Like everyone else, we purchased War Savings Bonds. We also saved aluminum foil from chewing gum wrappers and cigarette packages and rolled it into balls of many layers.

Because of the shortage of gas, car trips had to be restricted. Since our school was not able to supply buses for

Since our school was not able to supply buses for our girls' athletic teams, we had to rely on public transportation to go to our games.

our girls' athletic teams, we had to rely on public transportation to go to our games. Some of the other passengers were treated to our singing and loud laughter, particularly if we had won the game. As I recall, the school managed to transport the boys' teams to their games.

Oneida, Ltd., a maker of silverware, advertised extensively in magazines using the slogan, "Back Home for Keeps," featuring a returning serviceman enveloping his sweetheart. We girls cut out these ads and taped them to our locker doors. We could also send away to the company for large posters, which we taped about the locker room. The artist was Jon Whitcomb, a prolific magazine illustrator who served as a Navy artist in the Pacific Theater. Interestingly enough, I later married a John Whitcomb, but he was no relation.

An Oneida "Back Home for Keeps" poster

Some of our teachers had to work in defense factories at night, so their teaching during the day left something to be desired. Also, a number of male teachers enlisted and their replacements were poor. The boys' gym teacher and coach had worked with a minor league baseball team and he was not used to coaching high school boys. His swearing was a source of horror to us girls and was criticized by other faculty members and parents. Also, our substitute chemistry teacher was quite inexperienced and she caused a nasty explosion in the classroom, receiving bad burns on her arm. Fortunately there were no injuries to students.

When it was time for my sister to go to college, she had to choose by hearsay because there was no gasoline for trips to visit colleges. She decided on Oberlin College in Oberlin, Ohio, and had to make the trip alone by Pullman train. She had never traveled alone before and, of course, was apprehensive. The train went first to Cleveland where she collected her trunk and then she traveled by bus to Oberlin. It was quite an ex-

My husband tells the story of a friend in Maine who was out on the rocky coast with his girlfriend one night. Suddenly they spotted a small boat carrying two men come ashore.

Mernie (left) and sister Barbara at Avalon

perience for her. Oberlin, along with many other colleges, had a V-12 program which provided special training to naval and air corps units.

My family always spent summers at our shore house in Avalon, New Jersey. From our attic, we could see convoys of ships going by. During the war years the Avalon Beach Patrol acquired dogs to help protect the shoreline. While walking on the boardwalk at night, we would see the men and dogs searching the beaches. We understood they were looking for spies who could have been dropped off by enemy submarines or ships at sea. It was rumored that an enemy vessel was spotted just off the beach at a neighboring resort.

My husband tells the story of a friend in Maine who was out on the rocky coast with his girlfriend one night. Suddenly they spotted a small boat carrying two men come ashore. The couple alerted the authorities and the men were captured. They were indeed spies.

In Avalon, we were required to have blackout curtains so that not a bit of light could show outside. If we had to go out at night in the car, we were not to turn on our headlights. However, the top half of the headlights were painted black, just in case we needed lights in an emergency.

I recall one evening going with my mother and a friend to pick up my sister who worked at the local movie theater on the boardwalk. On the way home, we told mother she was driving on the wrong side of the road. She insisted she was not, but we felt certain she was. Finally we convinced her to flick on the lights for a brief second, and sure enough, she was hugging the left curb. It was scary.

I remember the joy and relief we felt on V-J Day. The word was out that the war was finally over! Church bells rang, and people flocked to churches to give thanks. I was waiting on tables at a hotel in Avalon when the news came. I went out on the fire escape and cried. I was so happy that my brother and my boyfriend would no longer have to fight!

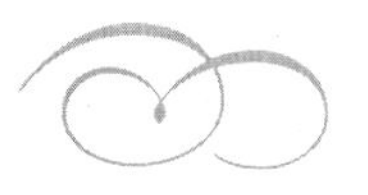

Ellen Petersen Richards

Ellen graduated from Dickinson College in Carlisle, Pennsylvania, with membership in Phi Beta Kappa. She and her husband live in Arlington, Virginia. Ellen has volunteered in political activities and was a docent in the Smithsonian Museum of Natural History.

During the war years, I was attending Prospect Park High School in southeastern Pennsylvania. The war was very real in our household, not only because of rationing, blackouts, and many other inconveniences, but because my two older brothers were both in the service.

My brother Richard enlisted in the Navy V-5 program in the spring of 1943 and spent the greater part of his service in flight training at Norman, Oklahoma, where he obtained his "Wings."

My brother Roger enlisted in the Army Specialized Training Program (ASTP), also in the spring of 1943. After military training, he was assigned to the 333rd Infantry Regiment of the 84th Division as a mortar gunner. His regiment went into action in November of 1944, in Heerlen, Holland, and continued across northwestern Europe, reaching the Elbe River by V-E Day May 8, 1945. In an autobiographical sketch, Roger tells of his war experiences. These include many battles with German troops, liberating French, British and American POWs from a concentration camp, processing thousands of German soldiers who surrendered to the Americans rather than being captured by the Russians, and playing in a jazz band while performing occupation duties.

At home, I recall an underlying tension most of the time. Daily war news was seldom discussed, and concern for Roger's safety was rarely mentioned. I do remember a brief sense of relief whenever a letter arrived with proof that he was alive and well.

My father was a mechanical engineer in the Stoker De-

The Petersen family 1943

Perhaps the biggest inconvenience was gas rationing, which prevented us from taking our biennial car trips to visit my grandparents in Iowa. We could not afford to travel by train.

partment of Westinghouse in Lester, Pennsylvania. Mother conscientiously saved rendered fat, which was collected at the butcher shop, and, of course, we were affected by the various food shortages and other inconveniences. It is a wonder our mothers were able to prepare nutritious and tasty meals on a daily basis. Perhaps the biggest inconvenience was gas rationing, which prevented us from taking our biennial car trips to visit my grandparents in Iowa. We could not afford to travel by train.

Another fact of life during the war years was air raid drills carried out under the supervision of volunteer civilian air raid wardens. During these exercises the wardens were responsible for seeing that residents in their assigned areas were complying with the publicized safety precautions. Between the sound of the warning siren and the all-clear siren, there was to be no visible light in houses, and no pedestrians or cars were to be out and about unless on official business.

Previous to one of the planned exercises, my friend Ruth Smith and I were asked if we would play the roles of "suspicious" characters trying to elude the air raid wardens as we wandered in the dark on a "mission." It sounded like fun so we agreed.

On the appointed evening we showed up at the firehouse headquarters for our instructions. We were told to stay within a reasonable distance from our starting place and we would be given a lead of five minutes before the wardens would start out to search for us.

The blackout siren soon sounded and off we went toward the railroad station. A right turn took us away from the main street at which point we became aware of the terrible darkness. With no streetlights on, no moon shining, and no audible sounds or movement, we felt a disturbing aloneness. However, thoughts came to mind of the wardens somewhere in the enveloping blackness starting their search for us, and we were determined to give them a challenge.

We rushed on for several more blocks before deciding we were easy prey since we were out in the open. An old house on the property where the elementary school now stands seemed like a good place to slip behind in order to assess our situation. We had no clue as to which direction the wardens went from the start of the chase, and we had no signs to indicate if they might be near us now. Remaining where we were might give us an answer as to our safest return route if we should finally hear someone. So we waited as the dark and si-

The Army announces that it is in urgent need of band instruments to outfit 800 Army bands overseas. The instruments will be paid for in cash by Army representatives at Macy's (Music Dept.), through April 21st, and at Abraham & Straus, in Brooklyn, from April 24th through the 28th.

Ad appearing in a Broadway playbill, 1945

Ellen in 1945

lent night continued.

The time for the all-clear siren was approaching as we set out to return warily in the direction of the firehouse. Just as we were able to see the outline of the building, the all-clear siren announced the end of the air raid and lights came on all over the town.

As we neared the firehouse, we could see a group of wardens who had already returned. We were greeted with the words, "Where in the world have you girls been? We had no idea where you were. Didn't you know you were supposed to stay out in plain view?" We apologized for our misunderstanding of the rules of the game, but found it difficult to understand why suspicious characters would have remained in plain view.

We never heard if our particular test was added to subsequent exercises—perhaps with a more clearly defined training objective. At any rate, we were not invited to participate again. Fortunately for all concerned, the wardens were never tested in a similar real life situation.

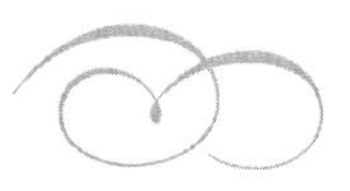

Dorothy Stroud Croney

Dorothy is active in her church, having sung in the choir forty-six years and having taught Sunday School forty years. She enjoys summers at Cape May, New Jersey, and is a Red Hatter.

I lived the first twelve years of my life in Chester, Pennsylvania, with my parents, my older brother, George, and my older sister, Jane. My father worked as an auditor for the Du Pont Company in Wilmington, Delaware. My mother was a housewife and taught Sunday School at the Providence Avenue Methodist Episcopal Church.

The plant made smokeless powder and TNT, and produced more than a billion pounds of explosives.

Dorothy (second row left) and her family in Louisville, Kentucky, 1943

In September of 1940, our family was suddenly uprooted when my father was transferred to Du Pont's Indiana Ordnance Works in New Albany, Indiana. He found a large house for us to rent one-half mile from Shawnee Park and one block from the Ohio River in Louisville, Kentucky. Mother, Jane, and I traveled down by train while our furniture and all our belongings were transported by a moving van, thanks to Du Pont.

Having just completed his internship in dermatology at Duke University in Durham, North Carolina, George went to University Hospital in Cleveland, Ohio, for his residency. A young college student who had developed a rash was sent to the hospital, and it was love at first sight for her and George. They were married shortly thereafter.

Daddy and Jane, then nineteen, both drove across the Ohio River every day to work at the Indiana Ordnance Works—my father as an auditor and Jane as a stenographer. The plant made smokeless powder and TNT, and produced more than a billion pounds of explosives. Jane and my father worked long hours every day, six or seven days a week.

I started seventh grade at Shawnee Junior High School where many of my classmates made fun of my Yankee accent. I was homesick for my old friends and didn't want to go to this new school. The first few weeks were rough, and sometimes I turned around and went home. Some days I didn't

Because of the cost, length of time needed, and the fact that most trains were being used for carrying troops, no one from the family could accompany Jane.

go at all. When the truant officer came to our house, Mother was at her wit's end. Finally, a kind neighbor made arrangements for one of the girls in our class to befriend me. We became fast friends, my homeroom was changed to hers, and I was soon a part of her group of friends. As it turned out, it was a wonderful three years.

Meanwhile, Jane had a great time dating Du Pont engineers, finally settling on one, a safety engineer, who was transferred in 1943 to the Hanford Engineer Works in Hanford, Washington. Du Pont operated this plant for the U.S. government for a fee of one dollar. We learned in 1945 that this plant had been mass-producing plutonium, a material then available only in a laboratory state. How big a job it was came to light only after Hiroshima, when the security curtain was partially lifted.

In 1943 both my father and Jane returned to the Wilmington office, and we returned to our home in Chester. I enrolled in Chester High School in September of 1943.

Jane's engineer friend wasn't about to let her go and made arrangements for a wedding in Washington on October 16. Remember, this was wartime and the only way to go to Richland, Washington, was by train. Because of the cost, length of time needed, and the fact that most trains were being used for carrying troops, no one from the family could accompany Jane, but arrangements were made for Du Pont friends to be on hand to take part in the ceremony.

My Chester High School boyfriend left school before graduation to join the Army Air Corps, and while still in school, he worked part time at the Sun Ship Building and Drydock Company. We exchanged class rings and wrote faithfully to one another for a year while he was in the Philippines, but upon his return, we realized the romance was at an end and we returned our rings.

Meanwhile, Mother and a neighbor thought it would be a good idea for me to write to the neighbor's son, a navigator on a B17 flying missions from England across the English Channel and very much in the thick of the war. When he returned home on leave (he was twenty and I was sixteen), there was much excitement in our household as we attempted to make me look and act more grownup. He took me to Philadelphia to the ballet and to fine restaurants, but I soon tired of this new life. I refused to go out again, turning back to my high school sweetheart. I recall hearing Mother and the navigator's mother discuss my immaturity on the telephone.

Aside from the ways the war affected my father's employment, friends' military service, and our home life, I recall little in the way of hardship, except for the inconvenience of food and gas rationing. Living in Louisville we had few concerns about security, as did the people living in coastal states. After all, we were only a few miles from Fort Knox, a huge Army base and home of the nation's gold.

Back in Chester, my cousin and a group of girls called "Control Center" met at a secret place in Chester Park. This is where air raid wardens and civil defense men reported while the girls operated telephones during drills. My cousin was also active in a program entertaining hospitalized veterans sponsored by Delaware County Girl Scout troops. I was involved in this as well.

I met my husband, Bud (Frank), in 1949 when he received an honorable discharge from the Navy, after serving six

Dorothy (right), author Peggy George (left) and friends, 1944

years as a sonarman on a subchaser in the Pacific. We married in 1950 and had two sons, Paul and David. Paul joined the Navy during the Vietnam War. Bud was forty-five when he died during heart bypass surgery in April of 1971. David was twelve at the time, and he and I took care of each other until Paul returned home in 1973.

In Louisville my mother had become active in the Girls Scouts of America. When we returned to Chester, she continued with this work, reactivating Girl Scouting in Chester and serving as District Chairman. It was she who enlisted the aid of virtually all Delaware County Girl Scout troops in programs for hospitalized veterans. Mother was dedicated to the Girl Scouts, her uniform becoming her everyday wardrobe.

A very special event occurred toward the end of the war when Mrs. Hewitt and my mother took Peggy and me by train to Philadelphia to see the show *Oklahoma*. How we loved it!

And now here it is the year 2005 and within a few weeks I will be taking my granddaughters, Amanda and Nicole, to the Du Pont Theater in Wilmington, Delaware, to see *Oklahoma* and to hear again the song, "I'm Just A Girl Who Can't Say No." I suspect they'll understand the meaning of the words far better than I did back in1944.

In spite of the horrors of war, the world seemed a much more innocent place than it does today.

Molly Fulton Trout

After returning from Germany with her parents, Molly graduated from Doylestown High School in Pennsylvania, married, and had six children. She pursued her own college interests after her children completed their schooling.

In 1941 my father was in the Civil Service working for the government as an architect at Fort Meyer, Virginia. When Pearl Harbor was attacked by the Japanese, he was put in charge of a map room where the location of all the American ships was plotted. While doing that job he was offered a commission as a First Lieutenant in the newly created Transportation Corps. Part of his responsibility was helping to prepare for the D-Day invasion. His operation was guarded by two servicemen and his daily reports were sent to the President and the Secretary of War. The actual morning of the invasion, after hearing the news on the radio, Mother awakened Daddy to tell him what had happened. He responded that he had known all about it well in advance.

Following D-Day, my father received a promotion to Captain and was sent to a post in Wales in Great Britain to help manage the shipment of troops and supplies in the European Theater. Mother remained in Arlington, caring for my brother and me.

In 1945 I was twelve years old. World War II ended and my father was transferred to Germany. At that point my mother, brother, and I were able to go to Germany to be with him. We sailed out of the New York harbor, landed at Bremerhaven, and then on to Frankfurt. I will never forget my first sight of Frankfurt, Germany. We came up a set of stairs into the city, and there was nothing but rubble. Everywhere I looked was desolation. Then I saw people actually coming out of the rubble, where they had sought shelter. Everyone carried a basket in which to place whatever objects or food they could find. I later learned that the British bombed at night and the Americans during the day.

We came up a set of stairs into the city, and there was nothing but rubble. Everywhere I looked was desolation.

My father was in charge of the port in Duisberg, and monitored all the barge traffic on the Rhine River. A great variety of goods traveled on barges on the Rhine. Often our family took trips on my father's boat as he inspected these barges. Along the Rhine we saw many small castles that had been tollbooths to collect tolls for shipping. In my twelve-year-old mind, the castles were for having dances which I attended in gorgeous clothes.

We lived in the beautiful home of a wealthy manufacturer. It was taken over by the United States, but would be returned to the owner's widow at a later date. Our house was staffed with maids, cooks, and chauffeurs. Daddy was just a Captain, but in order to help feed and clothe the German people, it was the policy of the United States to provide their officers with these workers, who also lived in the house.

One day the man who piloted my father's boat told me, "We will defeat you the next time." The maids and cooks all wanted nylon stockings. The young man that was a chauffeur had a lot of trouble with malaria and my mother would get medicine for him at the Post Exchange. He had been in Rommel's Africa Corps where he contracted malaria.

After living in Duisberg a year, we moved to Berlin. Daddy was assigned as the American liaison to the railroad system. The city had been divided into four sectors—British, Russian, French, and American—and he worked with the other countries in the movement of trains throughout the city.

We lived on Gary Strasse in another large house staffed with servants. Our home was in the British Zone of Berlin. Consequently, we met and socialized with many British soldiers. Although I had attended a British school in Duisberg, in Berlin I went to an American school, where I met many other American students. Sixty-six students attended this junior-senior high school.

Students at the American School in Berlin, Germany

On Friday evenings we went to free movies at Harnack House, a former meeting house for a German philosophical society named after Adolf von Harnack (1851-1930), a well-known German theologian. The movies were provided by the British Broadcasting Company and featured classics by Dickens and Shakespeare as well as comedy shows. Before the movie began, our family would often have dinner on the first floor of the building where there was a cafeteria for American officers and their dependents.

My mother and I frequently used bus transportation to get around Berlin. Since we spoke very little German, we sometimes had difficulty. We could easily sense that the German people did not like us.

One day we took a barge ride across a lake into Switzerland. It was such fun. The local people on the barge began singing various folk songs—the kind where one person sings the verse and the others respond with the chorus. It was so different from how we would behave in the United States where

I remember seeing the huge arena in Berlin where Hitler's troops paraded and sang "Deutschland Uber alles."

no one talks to anyone in such a setting.

One day my father had an army friend visiting. The neighborhood children started to walk around the American flag, which was flying from the flagpole in our front yard. They were chanting, "Heil Hitler." The visiting Colonel went outside and gently felt the children's arms and in German said, "Good children flesh—good for cooking." They ran home and we never saw them again.

When we took trips to Cologne or Frankfurt, we saw so much destruction. The original bridges had been destroyed and were temporarily replaced by pontoon bridges. The lovely Cologne Cathedral was blackened from fires. I remember seeing the huge arena in Berlin where Hitler's troops paraded and sang "Deutschland Uber alles."

My brother was two years old when we went to Germany. He liked to be in the kitchen with the cook, and he enjoyed being with the maids, gardener, and chauffeur. They made a fuss over him and he easily learned the language. Often he unwittingly acted as a translator for us. As fate would have it, he joined the infantry at age twenty-one and was sent to a post in Germany. His next post was where my father had begun his military career at Fort Meyer, Virginia where my brother served as a member of the ceremonial "Old Guard."

After two years in Germany, we came home to Pennsylvania. It was a joy to see the Statue of Liberty as our ship pulled into the New York harbor. We had sailed over and back

Molly's home in Duisberg, Germany

on troop ships and were quartered in small staterooms set aside for dependents. I often thought of those young men during the war who must have been so frightened as they set out for the unknown on these same ships.

Recently I went to France and saw the Normandy Beach area. What a hallowed place. The struggles our troops endured to defeat Germany is evident from remnants of concrete bunkers along the beaches. Today, whenever I see houses or factories being demolished, my mind goes back to the destruction I saw in Frankfurt, Cologne, and parts of Berlin. War does terrible things to people's lives.

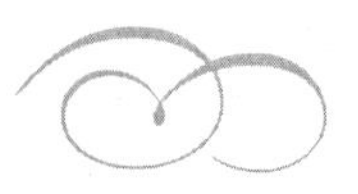

Carol Sandemar Connard

After twenty years of being a wife, homemaker, and mother of four, Carol graduated from Temple University with a B.A. in Early Childhood Education. For eighteen years she taught in a private school.

I grew up in Union, New Jersey. My father had come to this country from Sweden as a young man with a degree in drafting and had found work at the Elastic Stop Nut Company. The company made fasteners, which replaced rivets in joining together pieces of metal, such as airplane wings.

In the early 1940s the owner died, and after his wife sold out, the company was in turmoil. The owner's brother developed a similar product, had it patented, and opened his own company, Penn Engineering and Manufacturing Corporation in Doylestown, Pennsylvania. He asked my father to join him, which he did in 1942. My mother, brother and I remained in Union for a time.

Every Monday morning my father traveled from Union to Doylestown and came back Friday evening. Because of gas rationing, there were only a few cars on the highways. Several times my father was stopped by the police, and each time he had to show a special permit to prove he was purchasing gas necessary for the trip. Since the factory was making products for the war effort, there was no problem.

December 7, 1941 is very vivid in my mind. My grandparents, cousins, and other family members were together that Sunday afternoon in Union. As usual, all of us cousins were laughing, giggling, and having lots of fun. We were used to hearing the adults telling us to be quiet, but this particular Sunday, someone shouted, "Be quiet!" in such a way that we knew something momentous had happened.

We were used to hearing the adults telling us to be quiet, but this particular Sunday, someone shouted, "Be quiet!" in such a way that we knew something momentous had happened.

We stayed in Union for a year or so, coming down to Doylestown in the summers and living in a rented half-house. When I was in eighth grade, my parents found a house they liked, and they and my brother moved down. I stayed with friends until the end of the semester.

It was during those summer months that I learned to twirl a baton. Since we weren't attending school in Doylestown, we had few friends and it was lonely. I had seen a baton advertised on a cereal box, and decided to order one. I didn't even need to send money, only box tops. I asked a friend in Union to teach me how to twirl. She was a good teacher and I proved to be an apt student, spending much of my summer practicing.

When I started my freshman year in Doylestown, I decided to try out for majorette, even though I was only a freshman. Over one hundred girls were in the tryouts, but I soon realized I was much more proficient then most of them and, fortunately, I was selected. As a newcomer, it was a wonderful way to become a part of the school scene.

In school, we students collected scrap metal and bought war stamps. Each card had spaces in which to paste stamps worth twenty-five cents, which we purchased at the post office. When the card was full, the value was $18.75. Then we would turn in the card of stamps for a War Savings Bond, worth $25.00 in ten years.

Food rationing was a major fact of life during the war. Aside from sugar, butter, and meats, other rationed foods included dried peas and beans, frozen and canned fruits and vegetables, coffee, and many other products. Some items not requiring stamps were fresh fruits and vegetables, fish, cereal, and milk. Local newspapers ran notices advising the community which food products were available during a given week and which stamps were to be used.

My father had lots of friends and relatives still living in Sweden. As much as we had shortages of food here in the United States, it was nothing compared to what they had to endure. At Christmas time, he would send boxes packed with rice, coffee, and sugar to everyone he knew. They were so grateful.

Carol, the majorette

Of course there was no television, so we learned about the war from the radio and from a special news program at the movies called "The Eyes and Ears of the World," which reviewed the week's news. We always knew when it was about to come on because it had its own very special music. I can hear it now. Also, the program began with a newsreel spinning around.

Towards the end of my high school years, the male teachers began to return from the war. Until then, retired teachers and people not even certified were teaching in the classroom. When the veterans returned, the other people gradually left the schools and the veterans were shifted around into the subjects where they were best qualified. Sometimes they taught one subject for one marking period until another returning veteran took their place. Then they would teach a different subject. In one school year, I had six math teachers, one for each marking period.

Even though I had no immediate relatives in the war, I

UNITED STATES OF AMERICA
OFFICE OF PRICE ADMINISTRATION

195704 U

WAR RATION BOOK No. 3 *Void if altered*

NOT VALID WITHOUT STAMP

Identification of person to whom issued: PRINT IN FULL

MARTHA. R. NICE
(First name) (Middle name) (Last name)

Street number or rural route 128 Glencoe Road

City or post office Upper Darby State Pa.

AGE	SEX	WEIGHT	HEIGHT	OCCUPATION
66	Female	180 Lbs.	5 Ft. 8 In.	Housewife

SIGNATURE Martha R. Nice.
(Person to whom book is issued. If such person is unable to sign because of age or incapacity, another may sign in his behalf.)

WARNING
This book is the property of the United States Government. It is unlawful to sell it to any other person, or to use it or permit anyone else to use it, except to obtain rationed goods in accordance with regulations of the Office of Price Administration. Any person who finds a lost War Ration Book must return it to the War Price and Rationing Board which issued it. Persons who violate rationing regulations are subject to $10,000 fine or imprisonment, or both.

LOCAL BOARD ACTION

Issued by .... (Local board number) (Date)

Street address ....

City .... State ....

.... (Signature of issuing officer)

OPA Form No. R-130

Book 4

War ration book

recall the night it ended. Everyone was out on the streets celebrating—shouting, blowing horns, and dancing. I had never seen anything like it before, and I have never seen anything like it since.

Molly Leatherman Trout

Molly's father was a grocery store manager and her mother a schoolteacher. She and her husband, her high school sweetheart, have three daughters. Molly loves Doylestown, Pennsylvania, and can't imagine living anywhere else.

I was still quite young during the war years but, like everyone else, I knew we were at war.

My father had been managing food stores since he was nineteen, but when the war broke out he and many others in the area went to work in defense plants. He worked at the Rohm and Haas plant in Bristol, Pennsylvania, where they made Plexiglas for airplanes. I can still remember how smelly his clothes and lunch box were when he arrived home in the evening.

After a few years at Rohm and Haas, Daddy returned to the grocery store business, first managing a co-op food store at 68 South Main Street (now Sabine Rose Gallery) in Doylestown, and later buying out the owners. He worked long hours in the store and had to spend much time just on record keeping, including the whole business of food rationing stamps. In spite of what friends suggested, our family never took advantage of his position with food. We ate rationed food, the same as everyone else, although we did have first choice.

Living with rationed sugar was difficult for our family. Mother tried using a liquid sweetener, a kind of syrup. It tasted terrible, so very quickly, we went back to our limited supply of sugar.

> ***The air raid siren went off when we were on the school bus returning home from school. We had to get out of the bus and hide in the woods.***

Molly's father's store at 68 South Main Street

Sometimes I would go with mother to the Red Cross office where a group of women gathered to wrap bandages and do other assigned tasks. The outings were sort of a social time for the women, as well as a time to perform tasks for the war effort. Mother also knit some kind of thing that went on the wrist. And she and Daddy had a Victory Garden from which she was able to do some canning.

In school, we had air raid alerts when we had to scrunch down under our desks. One day, the air raid siren went off when we were on the school bus returning home from school. We had to get out of the bus and hide in the woods.

Aside from these occasional air raid alerts, school activities went on very much as usual. My boyfriend, now my husband of fifty-two years, played guard on the football team. He was No. 38. I was a cheerleader, cheering Doylestown High on to victory.

The Red Cross sometimes called on us girls who had recently graduated from high school to attend activities for returning servicemen. One time we visited the Valley Forge General Hospital to play cards with the men in the tuberculosis ward where we had to wear masks. The nurses told us it was to protect the men from getting whatever germs we might have. I wonder.

A highlight of these activities for returning servicemen occurred at the home of Oscar Hammerstein here in Doylestown. We were to play cards, dance, and sing with sailors from the Philadelphia Naval Base.

Molly (second from left) cheering Doylestown High on to victory

This was in 1951. *South Pacific*, by Richard Rodgers and Oscar Hammerstein, had opened on Broadway April 7, 1949. It is based on James Michener's *Tales of the South Pacific*, which was awarded the Pulitzer Prizes for both Drama and Literature in 1950. The original cast included Mary Martin as a U.S. Navy nurse who falls in love with a middle-aged French plantation owner played by opera star Ezio Pinza.

The Red Cross sometimes called on us girls who had recently graduated from high school to attend activities for returning servicemen.

It so happened that while we were at Mr. Hammerstein's home, Mary Martin, her husband, and daughter, Heller, were on a cross-country motor trip and stopped to see her good friend, Oscar Hammerstein. She wore a brown linen dress and had short curly hair, just as in the play. Everyone wanted her to perform and she obliged. She kicked off her shoes and entertained us all by "washing that man right out of her hair." What an unexpected treat!

This all occurred after the war, but I do remember V-J Day. Our family was at Bayshore, New Jersey, along with my

Jacket for the soundtrack of South Pacific

It so happened that while we were at Mr. Hammerstein's home, Mary Martin, her husband, and daughter, Heller, were on a cross-country motor trip and stopped to see her good friend, Oscar Hammerstein.

grandmother and aunt. When the news came over the radio, we packed up and went to Asbury Park where we knew there would be more action. There we joined in the celebration, with horns blowing and dancing in the street.

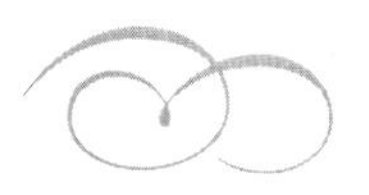

Anna Elizabeth Shaddinger

May 25, 1903-November 12, 2003
(as told to the author in 1999)

Anna was a very spirited person and a woman ahead of her time. She made life-long friendships wherever she went. Her memory served her well for 100 years.

WORLD WAR I

During the war years, everyone was knitting. I couldn't knit and since Grandma was left-handed, she couldn't teach me. I decided to go to the Armory where they were giving out free needles and yarn to people making knitted articles for servicemen. They showed me how to "knit two, pearl two" for the wristlets they needed. Hattie Lear, a teacher friend of Mama, taught me to make socks. I made seven or eight pairs.

Of course, I remember the white oleo and the little orange button that you squeezed into the oleo to make it turn yellow.

We bought our groceries at the old Acme where the Doylestown Inn now stands. Mr. Paist, who married Reba Colby, sat in a little box and took your money.

And every day the paper would carry deaths and other reports about the servicemen. Sometimes they would print their letters, which they wouldn't do today because it would be too much like printing local news.

Mrs. Freeman, our pastor's wife, made candy for all the people who went into the service. We had women going too, mostly as nurses. Lots of people would go to the train station to see them off, and Mrs. Freeman would hand each soldier and nurse a box of her homemade candy.

> ***Lots of people would go to the train station to see them off, and Mrs. Freeman would hand each soldier and nurse a box of her homemade candy.***

With the shortage of food, Victory Gardens sprung up all over. Burpee Seed Company set aside land for people to grow food. Grandpop dug up the whole back yard and planted potatoes.

There were rallies to sell war bonds and they had musicals at the Court House. Frank Gerlitzki led music and one of the Holkey boys organized mouth organ bands.

On Armistice Day I was home sick with the flu. So many people had the flu and doctors were scarce because of the war. I had been sick for six weeks, but when the church bells rang and the fire whistle blew, I decided I had to go up town to be a part of the celebration. I was so weak. I remember sitting down to rest on the steps of Clymer's Department Store.

Then the boys came home. There were weddings and everyone was so happy. At church, we had a big discussion on how we would honor the servicemen and the one woman who had served. Finally, it was decided to put up a plaque, which you can see as you enter the church.

That was World War I. Now for World War II. I hope I don't live to see anymore wars.

During the war years there was no gas for traveling.

WORLD WAR II

It was back in 1944, a year before the end of the war that I got this idea that I would like to start a craft shop during the summer months. It would be a good break from teaching first graders, and because of the gas shortage, I couldn't travel.

I had always liked crafts and doing things with my hands. I particularly liked working in clay, but had never really learned how to make ceramic objects. There was another teacher in our school who made such lovely things and I asked her if she would teach me. So she did. At first, she didn't have a kiln so we had to take our things to Ottsville to be fired. Then my friend, Anna, decided to buy her own kiln.

It was during the war years and, of course, there was no gas for traveling. Since we couldn't travel around the country, we thought it might be fun to go someplace to set up a shop and sell our things. Working through the winter, we had accumulated quite a supply of handcrafted objects.

I had been to Hampton Beach, New Hampshire, several years earlier on my way back from Quebec with the other first grade teacher and my friend Bertha Worman. We spent a week there for $1.00 a night in a room right across from the beach. We loved it. There were little shops along the street just across from the ocean and there was no boardwalk then. There were a lot of wartime factories in the area and the Navy Yard was just across the river in Portsmouth, so we thought that there were plenty of people in the area who might want to buy our handmade articles.

The day after school let out—remember there was no gas—we decided to go to Hampton Beach to get a lay of the land. We took a night bus to Boston and then a bus or train—I forget—the rest of the way. I had written in advance to the man who owned a hotel and who was president of the Chamber of Commerce, asking him if there were any ceramic shops in Hampton Beach. He thought ceramics was something to eat.

When we arrived, a real estate man picked us up in his car and showed us a number of shops for rent, all of them too grandiose for us. We decided to walk back to the hotel to take a look for ourselves at some other places.

Along the main street of shops across from the beach, we came to this place that was really just a window, next to a tearoom. That's all it was, a window with a little room behind it. But we thought we could open the window and put our things on a shelf and just sell from there.

Anna's "store" in New Hampshire

The owner of the tearoom also owned this window. We went to see him but he, too, thought that ceramics was a food and was dubious about having a shop that would be in competition with him. When we showed him how we could help each other out, he rented it to us for $300 for the season.

Our landlord then found us a glass showcase, which fit into the window on a little platform. As time went on, our only objection was a fireplug right by our window, where people would sit to rest.

But we were content with our decision. I remember

thinking at the time, "There's a divinity that shapes our ends, Rough hew them how we will—" [Hamlet, Prince of Denmark, Act V, Scene 2].

After renting our shop, we had to find a place to live. We talked to Mr. Goding at the hotel, but that would be too expensive for us, so we walked back into the village just behind the street where the shops were. All of the rooms we looked at were just unsealed attics, which would never do. We saw a woman sweeping a sidewalk and we told her we were looking for a place to stay. She said she had a friend who rented out rooms, so she phoned her right then. The woman had some cousins visiting but they were just leaving and she said she would be happy to show us the place. She came to pick us up fifteen minutes later in front of Howard Johnson's.

That's how Edna Kimball walked into my life. She had the heart the size of four people. Her place was one-half mile from the ocean and one mile from the shop. There was a bus available. She would charge $13 a week for both of us. I can still remember the first time I saw the room. It was a big bedroom with two big beds and pretty white curtains swaying gently from the ocean breeze. Well, we took it.

We headed home Sunday with plans to return later that week. School was out and the season had already begun, so we wanted to get started as soon as we could.

Anna as a young woman

Before we left, we looked at our shop again to see what we would need to clean it up. We saw a man painting outside and we asked if he had any extra paint. He gave us some in order for us to paint the inside of our shop.

We arrived home Monday and then had to figure out how we would be able to get gas to travel back. Anna and I had lots to pack. Our plan was for her to drive up to my house from her home in Drexel Hill and we would travel up in my car.

As soon as I got home, I went to see old Mr. Molloy at the Ration Board and told him that we were opening this shop and had to have just enough gas to get to New Hampshire. He said, "It seems more people are planning to open up shops. You don't think it's a gimmick just to get more gas, do you?" I explained that it really was so in our case. He asked how much gas I would need and gave me the needed ration stamps.

Meantime, lots of friends called to say that we could sell their handwork. Mrs. Steely said that we could sell her things for the church, and that I should do

"It seems more people are planning to open up shops. You don't think it's a gimmick just to get more gas, do you?"

We were there for V-J Day. The people went wild. Shopkeepers boarded up their places for fear of damage and everyone was dancing in the streets.

what the Women's Exchange in Jenkintown, Pennsylvania did: keep 30% for expenses and the rest would go to the person who made the handwork. I also had things from Mama and a number of her friends from church. One of the women made these scuffs—slippers—and we had darners that another friend made. They were little packets to take on trips in case you needed to darn anything. The people up there loved them, calling them "donners." One of my friends edged lace handkerchiefs with tatting and we sold them for $1.00. During the course of the summer, Mrs. Steeley couldn't make her dolls fast enough. They were sold as soon as we got a shipment from her.

We packed as much as we could and the rest we sent by Express. All summer, people would send the stuff they made. We didn't have much room in our shop, but we kept the things in our big apartment and would take things to the shop every day.

The first week we stayed open on Sunday because everyone else did. We decided that we had more lookers than buyers and that it was not worth staying open on Sunday. Mr. McKean, the owner, said that we had to stay open, but we said that we wouldn't. And we didn't. We put a sign on our window saying that we would be back Monday and hoped that people would come back then. If we could manage to get gas, we would travel around by car; if not, we would go by bus. I don't know how we got gas. Some of the people would just give us coupons and off we would go.

Some days if it was very hot and we wanted to go in the ocean, we would get out our "Be back tomorrow" sign and off we'd go to the ocean. Even though our little room behind the window was very small, we could change into our bathing suits there.

There was a band at Hampton Beach all summer. They would put on concerts three times a day—once in the afternoon and twice in the evening. People up there thought we were very clever. Our main ceramic objects were pieces of jewelry. This man from the band who played the violin came to us and asked if we could make earrings in the shape of a violin. So I said that we could. Anna said, "Why did you tell him that? How can we make them?" Well, I made a paper design and fooled around with the design and the clay and came up with a pair of violin earrings. I didn't think they were particularly good but the violinist was thrilled with them. He showed them to the other band players and one of them came to us to ask us to fix the broken hinge on his glasses.

Meanwhile Miss Kimball took good care of us. She made us our breakfast every day. Then we grabbed a hamburger for lunch and had our dinner at a restaurant for $5.00 a week.

By the end of the third or fourth week, we had our rent paid. Since we didn't have anything to worry about financially, we would take off when we wanted to. We took orders from people who were there vacationing and mailed the orders to them later. We had our kilns with us so we could make the jewelry in our room or in the shop.

Once a week, I would go to the beach early and write up the checks for all of the women back home. Then we would go to the bank in Exeter and arrive back at the shop to open at 10.00 a.m.

We had such a good time that we decided to go back the following year. In preparation, we went to New York to shop for our materials and made lots of things during the winter months.

In our first year, we had gone to Portsmouth to the New Hampshire League of Arts and Crafts show. We asked about joining the League. They said you needed eight weeks residency and your work had to pass a jury. The next year we submitted our application and were accepted.

The show that year was in Wolfboro. We didn't know who would take care of our shop. So I wrote to Mama, asking if she and one of her friends could come by train to help out, and they did.

We had another great year. We really sold stuff! I think that Mrs. Steeley and the other ladies had enough money from their handcrafts to pay off the remaining $2,500 on the mortgage at church. That's hard to believe but I think that is right. People loved the "donners."

Mrs. McKean, the landlord's wife, was one of our best customers. I was up there when he died about ten years ago. She was happy when I stopped over. She said he always remembered that we took off on Sundays.

We were there for V-J Day. The people went wild. Shopkeepers boarded up their places for fear of damage and everyone was dancing in the streets. I remember Leo the cook was dancing with anyone who would dance with him. There was a community church service. Back then everyone wore hats to church, so we wore the little crocheted hats that one of our women had made.

By the end of the second summer, we had each cleared $300. Anna was ready to stop. Now that the war was over and you could get gas again, she wanted to do more traveling. So I had to give it up. But, oh, we had such fun!

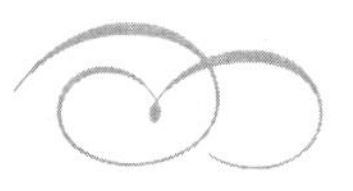

Louisa Skoog Whitten

Lee is a retired legal secretary. She spends much of her time reminiscing, painting, writing, dozing, and, with God's help, keeping out of trouble.

WORLD WAR I

I was born in Shawagunk, New York, in 1912, on a small farm. After a couple years, my parents moved to northern New Jersey, where Dad was caretaker of an estate high on a hill above Sterling. World War was raging in Europe, and one of my childhood memories is of a terrific explosion, said to be an ammunitions factory in the town of Elizabeth (or maybe Perth Amboy), which was visible from our apartment on the estate.

As the United States became more involved in the war, it was necessary for my father to register for the draft, and he was assigned to the cavalry. Fortunately, he never had to serve because of his work on the farm and his age. My Uncle Albert, however, did serve. He was a handsome young man whom I liked very much. I insisted on having my picture taken with him as he left early one morning to report to Fort Dix. My Aunt Ruth and he were married in Virginia before he was shipped overseas. In Europe he was a motorcycle dispatcher. Although he survived the bullets passing through the motorcycle, he did suffer the effects of gassing.

Lee (right) with her Uncle Albert

Eventually our family moved to Plainfield, New Jersey. I was only a child of six when the war ended, but I have a few memories of those years. A particular image that remains with me is of people gathering coal along railroad tracks since coal was very scarce. There was a lot of activity for the war effort. Even children were knitting mittens, scarves, and sweaters for the soldiers.

A particular image that remains with me is of people gathering coal along railroad tracks since coal was very scarce.

Once again, there was an explosion in Perth Amboy, also said to be from an ammunition factory. My father then found work in an airplane factory in Rahway, New Jersey and rode his motorcycle there from Plainfield every day. The planes were made partly with canvas, which caused my father to wonder that they could actually fly.

Rationing and shortages were felt in our home. Instead of butter, we used white margarine with the little red button you could squeeze to make the white turn to yellow. Sugar and flour I think were rationed, and we bought them in large containers whenever available.

We had to declare how much canned goods we had on hand. If we had a large quantity, even home-canned, we received fewer stamps.

Armistice Day came November 11, 1918. The war to end all wars was over!

WORLD WAR II

I was married in 1939 and moved to a small bungalow owned by my father-in-law, on Swamp Road near Doylestown, Pennsylvania. My husband was 4-F because of a fractured skull, caused by a horse kicking him in the head when he was young.

My husband's brother-in-law was killed in a railroad accident and three of his sister's four sons went off to war. The oldest was called near the end of the war, but did not have to go. The second son was in the Air Force, and he later told of dropping bombs on a huge railway center in Berlin. He came home from the war very upset and very negative about war. The two remaining sons were delivery boys for Western Union in Roanoke, Virginia, where their mother had moved. They enlisted when the war began, one lying about his age. One of the brothers joined the Navy, serving on a repair ship in the Pacific where he repaired some of the ships bombed at Pearl Harbor. The other son received an education while in the service and trained young soldiers. He served in France, in Italy, and also in Vietnam. Later he was stationed at the Pentagon, finally achieving the rank of colonel.

Lee with daughter Karen

Meanwhile at home, we listened to Ernie Pyle's radio reports of the soldiers at the front. I wrote letters to my nephews, which they said they appreciated. I was working as a secretary in the law firm of Ross and Russ until my daughter was born in 1943. For the next six years I stayed home, except for part-time jobs in a children's shop and in a law office.

Once again, rationing was a fact of life. Not only food, but shoes, tires, and gasoline were included. We had to declare how much canned goods we had on hand. If we had a large quantity, even home-canned, we received fewer stamps. I canned lots of fruits and vegetables and gave some to an old Irish family down the road. I made towels and clothing out of flour sacks. Some of the material was really very nice. I wanted to buy little white shoes for my daughter, but all I could find were shoes made out of paper. Her first good pair of shoes were brown, which I hated. I didn't want to put brown shoes on my little girl.

The war effort was in full force. I took a course to repair motor vehicles. In case there would be an emergency, I would be able to change tires and spark plugs and do a few other things. Since we had blackouts at night (black curtains on the windows and no street lights), I had to learn to drive in the dark, again in case I was needed in an emergency. We heard that German submarines were off the Atlantic coast, and who knew when we could be attacked? Actually, I dreamed of Japanese planes flying over the house and landing in the field. I also took a first-aid course, and learned how to bandage legs and arms, and how to stop bleeding. I'm sure these efforts would be of little use in the event of a real attack.

My parents were both from Sweden. During the war, Mother would send packages of sugar, coffee, and other food to our relatives in Sweden whenever possible.

Living on a farm, we survived comfortably in spite of rationing, but it was a happy day when the war ended and the lights came on again.

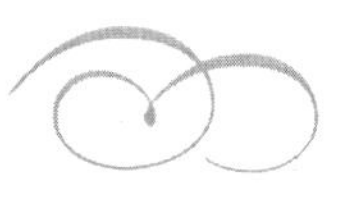

Myrtle George Nase

Myrtle was born in Trumbauersville, Bucks County, Pennsylvania. An elementary school teacher for many years, she and her husband now live in Sellersville, Pennsylvania. They have two daughters and five grandchildren.

I was living in Perkasie, Pennsylvania, during the war years. I had two babies—one in October 1942, the other in January 1945. My husband was a high school teacher and coach.

We had ration stamps for all kinds of things. One category was for fuel oil to heat our homes. Since there were small children in our home, we were issued extra stamps. Most people were given A stamps for gasoline, which provided just a few gallons a week to keep cars going. Teachers on high school staffs who hauled athletes to games, such as my husband, were given B stamps. Trolleys and trains were used much more than in previous times. Sugar, meat, coffee, and butter were also rationed. We ate lots of hot dogs back then, and oleomargarine. It was white but the package had a little red button that you squeezed. You would knead the package so the color would spread throughout and it would turn yellow. You had to keep kneading so that the oleo wasn't all streaked.

Myrtle with daughter Nancy

I never felt we were short of food or other necessities, but we did have to improvise sometimes. Victory Gardens sprung up everywhere. Since fresh food was at a premium, we used lots of canned products, and then we would take the lids off both ends, step on the cans and recycle them. All of these products—fuel oil, gasoline, and food products—were in great demand for our troops.

People were encouraged to buy War Savings Bonds and Stamps in order to provide the government with funds for the war.

People were encouraged to buy War Savings Bonds and Stamps in order to provide the government with funds for the war. The cheapest bond was $18.75 and if held to maturity in ten years would be worth $25.00. Stamps in various denominations were also sold, mostly to schoolchildren. The stamps were placed on a card which, when filled with twenty-five cent stamps, would be worth $18.75. Then, it could be turned in for a bond. Everyone, including schoolchildren, participated in the war effort.

We had blackouts when the

Just about every family had someone in the service. First my sister went off to be an Army nurse and was sent to the Panama Canal Zone. Then my brother was drafted into the Army.

fire siren would blow. Actually these were practice air raid drills. We never were really threatened in our area, but when the siren went off, we had to pull down the shades and stay inside. Civilian air raid wardens were the only ones out on the streets.

Teachers rationed stamps to people. The schools were issued stamps by the municipal officials, and people were told to report to a certain school to pick up their stamps. Here, teachers would be on duty to process the stamps. Every member of the family was given a book for each of the categories of rationed food. Keeping track of your stamps was sometimes confusing for the housewife. After distributing stamps to all the qualified people, the schools then had to burn the leftover stamps.

Just about every family had someone in the service. First my sister went off to be an Army nurse and was sent to the Panama Canal Zone. Then my brother was drafted into the Army near the close of the war. Fortunately, the war ended before he had to go abroad.

It was a glorious day when the war came to a close and families were once again reunited.

Don't Let That Shadow Touch Them
Buy WAR BONDS

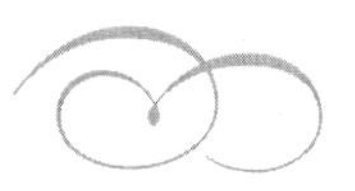

Rachel Lyne Jorgensen

Rachel and her husband now live in Iowa near their children. Among her other activities, she has enjoyed working in hospital admissions, lobbying on Capitol Hill with AAUW (American Association of University Women), traveling, and reading.

I grew up in Shepherdstown, West Virginia. The major impact of the war in our small town was the various shortages. Meat was scarce, but other than that, we seemed to manage in spite of rationing. My father was head cashier in the local bank, which was not far from home, so even gas rationing did not affect him greatly. And when bank employees went off to war, it seemed there was always someone to fill the vacancy. I remember Mother knitting long white strips, which were used as bandages.

I entered The College of William and Mary in Williamsburg, Virginia, in September of 1941. It was in December of that year that Pearl Harbor was attacked, and the United States was at war. It was here that the war became more real to all of us as many of the college men went off to war. As each man left, his name would be called out in the dining hall. If he had a girl friend, there would be a scream in response. During the course of my four years of college, a number of former students were killed in the line of duty.

Rachel, 1942

We had frequent air raid drills, and we had wooden boxes filled with sand in the hallways. The sand was to be used to extinguish fires caused by possible bomb explosions. Since we were close to Norfolk, we felt a real sense of danger, and some of us students took turns plane spotting from the library windows.

As each man left, his name would be called out in the dining hall. If he had a girl friend, there would be a scream in response.

There were very few male students remaining on campus: just the ones not eligible to serve or those receiving deferments because of their field of study.

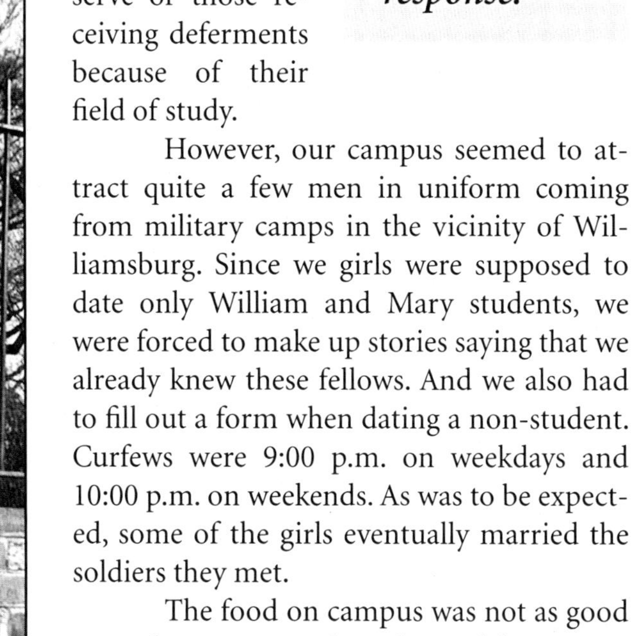

However, our campus seemed to attract quite a few men in uniform coming from military camps in the vicinity of Williamsburg. Since we girls were supposed to date only William and Mary students, we were forced to make up stories saying that we already knew these fellows. And we also had to fill out a form when dating a non-student. Curfews were 9:00 p.m. on weekdays and 10:00 p.m. on weekends. As was to be expected, some of the girls eventually married the soldiers they met.

The food on campus was not as good once the war started, and travel home was difficult due to gas rationing. The trains and buses were crowded. One time the college resurrected an old bus to take students to Washington, D.C., so the students could take trains home from there. However, once the bus warmed up, cockroaches appeared from every crevice and everyone was screaming and swatting bugs.

Once the bus warmed up, cockroaches appeared from every crevice and everyone was screaming and swatting bugs.

We had other shortages, also. We couldn't get nylon stockings, so sometimes we would paint our legs tan. Since elastic was scarce, half-slips buttoned at the waist.

After graduating from college, I thought it would be exciting to live in New York City and so I bought my train ticket and off I went, not knowing a soul. I soon found work at Gimbel's Department Store in the Accounting Department.

When the war ended, I went to Central Park where everyone was celebrating with music and dancing. I remember dancing with a soldier. What a joyful time it was.

Shortly after that, I met an Air Force veteran who also worked at Gimbel's. He was selling record players. And that's how I met Bill, now my husband of fifty-nine years.

ARE YOU
DOING ALL YOU CAN?

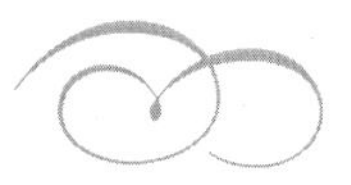

Gloria Braymeyer Brunner

Gloria is a retired nurse, living in a retirement community. She has four children and nine grandchildren, and enjoys reading and gardening.

I went into the Nurse Cadet Corps in August of 1945 at St. Luke's Hospital in Bethlehem, Pennsylvania. Because of the tremendous shortage of nurses during the war, the government paid all the expenses involved in our training. The commitment on our side was to serve wherever the country needed us at the time of our graduation. Since the war ended just as we completed our training, the only commitment required of us was to serve in the Army for a period of six months or to remain in the hospital that trained us for a period of two years. Not everyone fulfilled the commitment since some of the cadets married and even had children. I stayed with the hospital, although I am sorry now that I didn't go into the Army.

Gloria in 1948

Our training was intense. After the first three months, we were working on the wards. After the first year, we frequently worked the wards ourselves at night with minimum supervision. There was no time for slacking off in the hospital. We members of the Cadet Corps had to learn fast. We were given responsibilities and we were expected to make wise decisions.

There was no time for slacking off in the hospital. We members of the Cadet Corps had to learn fast.

We lived at the hospital and moved between two buildings depending on which shift we were working. Each time we moved we would have a different roommate. One of the buildings was the Bishop Thorpe Nursing Home, which has now been torn down. It was quiet there and no one would disturb our sleeping when we were on the night shift. It was the nicer of the two buildings. The other building was the Victoria White, named for the Director of Nursing long ago. It was a very old building.

Our attire changed every so often. The first few months we wore uniforms without caps, black shoes, and black stockings. Our uniforms were blue and white stripes with an apron. A few months into our training, we received caps. In our third year we received white shoes and white stockings. And, finally, after completing three years of training, we went into our white uniforms.

We worked very hard and were so glad when Friday afternoon rolled around. We would dart out the door and

Our little neighborhood was greatly affected by the war. Two of the boys died, and gold stars were placed in the windows of their homes.

head for the movies. On our way, we purchased hot dogs and ate on the run. I think the movies cost fifteen cents. We had to be back at the hospital by 7:30 p.m. and lights out by 9:00 p.m.

A few months before graduation we were allowed to move home. What a wonderful feeling to grab my things and head for home. I had had an intense three years. Yes, along with receiving a free education we were given fifteen dollars a month the first year of training, twenty dollars the second year, and thirty dollars the third year. We had three weeks off every summer. Other than that, we worked year round.

After passing the state board examinations, I received my R.N. and continued working at St. Luke's Hospital in Bethlehem.

My mother worked as a telephone operator and volunteered as an airplane spotter. My father worked at Bethlehem Steel and was an air raid warden. When that air raid siren went off, we all went to the nearest safe place immediately. No one was out on the street. And my father had a huge vegetable garden, which produced a large quantity of food for him and my mother to can—enough to hold us for a good while into the winter months.

Our little neighborhood was greatly affected by the war. Two of the boys died, and gold stars were placed in the windows of their homes. Two other servicemen came home

Cadet Nurse Recruiting Poster

paraplegics. Both my brothers served—one in the South Pacific and one in the European Theater. Mother worried constantly about them.

Of course, we had rationing. Everyone did, and no one complained. We were all at war and we all knew it. Because of the shortage of silk and nylon for stockings, we applied a liquid tan to our legs. If it rained, our "stockings" would run.

The radio played a big role in our lives as we listened to the music of Glenn Miller and the other Big Bands. And on both Pearl Harbor Day and D-Day, families sat quietly around the radio, eager for every bit of news about our servicemen. But on V-J Day, everyone was out on the streets. We cadets left the nurses' home and walked all over Bethlehem to join with everyone else in celebrating the end of the war.

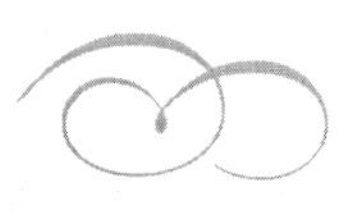

Margaret (Peggy) Carroll O'Neill

Peggy, an eighty year old mother and grandmother, retired after thirty-seven years pioneering and administering Bucks County's (Pennsylvania) services for the aging, and is now a freelance columnist.

When you approach your eightieth year of life, rivers of memories roll by and you find yourself remembering certain times by specific incidents or occasions, and so it is with memories of World War II.

I was in my teens at the time, attending Hallahan Catholic Girls High School in Philadelphia. The school's major war efforts were many. I have kept my Silver Sands 1943 yearbook. On the back page is shown a photograph, "A Good Buy." It is an airplane named "Hallahan," bought by the girls with $800,000 worth of savings bonds and stamps, along with $3,100 for Mass kits for Catholic chaplains. Additionally, a donation of $985.39 was made to the Red Cross, which also had thanked the girls for making sixty-eight afghans. All of this in a time when money was very scarce.

On Friday nights, we girls from Hallahan, along with others, happily answered the call to duty as we served refreshments, talked, played games, and danced with soldiers at the Philadelphia YMCA canteen. Strict rules were in place, and it was made clear to us that we were not at the canteen to find ourselves boyfriends. Although we were having fun, we knew our country was at war. The real horror of the war was not yet a reality and it was only later that many of those same soldiers were fighting and dying on the beaches of Normandy.

On Friday nights, we girls from Hallahan, along with others, happily answered the call to duty as we served refreshments, talked, played games, and danced with soldiers at the Philadelphia YMCA canteen.

Peggy (second from left), Chief Justice of Student Council

My mother invited one of the young men to our home for dinner. He was an Army medic from Chicago. I recall his arriving very sunburned to our home one Sunday. He told us they had been training on the New Jersey beaches. He later wrote to our family informing us he had been wounded in the Normandy invasion.

I graduated from high school in 1943 and took advantage of a program offered to good math students. For the last three months of our final year, we took special training at Temple University and the Frankford Arsenal, a large Army facility in the Northeast section of Philadelphia. This training resulted in my work-

The war years produced many women represented by the poster of Rosie the Riveter. In the Fire Control Experimental Shop, young girls learned how to run lathes and other machines to do their part for defense.

ing at the Arsenal as a Junior Engineer in the Fire Control Section. For all the training in drafting I had received, my actual work was sitting at a desk all day tracing drawings. I hated the job, mostly because it was boring and I couldn't talk to anyone.

One day a typist was needed to replace a woman who had gone on her honeymoon. I volunteered and became a secretary where my work was much more interesting and I could talk with other people. It was much later that I realized we had been involved in the Manhattan Project and the building of the atomic bomb.

As I think back on the decision to accept the training at Temple and the Arsenal, I believe a college education immediately after high school would have been the wiser choice. But back then it was not considered so important for the girls in the family to go to college and I had no encouragement from my family.

The war years produced many women represented by the poster of Rosie the Riveter. In the Fire Control Experimental Shop, young girls learned how to run lathes and other machines to do their part for defense. What fun we had on Friday afternoons when the girls in the office and the girls in the shop went horseback riding together in Pennypack Park. I was

The airplane named "Hallahan"

a terrible rider and ended up being bitten, kicked, and thrown by horses. There were other nights when we all went to The Little Rathskeller, a famous Philadelphia nightclub, and partied. We did not yet comprehend how the war was to affect us all—for the rest of our lives.

I continued to work at the Arsenal for about five years. My boss was a physicist, brilliant and eccentric, of Russian Jewish parentage. While working there, I was secretly questioned about him by the Arsenal Security. Sometime later, when I was married and living in Langhorne, Pennsylvania, someone from the FBI followed up on questions but did not reveal why. I always wondered if he had really been a spy.

At our home in Mayfair, my father worked as an insurance agent during the day but at night he left home to serve as a member of the Coast Guard Reserve. His job was to guard boats at the Philadelphia harbor.

Our pet dog was big and brown and beautiful and a wonderful watchdog, but he could not be trusted around strangers. He even bit my cousin. So our family got the idea that Mickey, our German Shepherd, could also do his part in the war. My father enrolled him in the Coast Guard and Mickey left home to patrol foreign beaches. My heart was broken on his leaving, but I can still remember how proud I was of my pet when he was killed in action. We received notification and an award from the Coast Guard as if he were a person.

The war continued and we saw our loved ones go off to foreign places—my brother to Germany and France, and my husband-to-be to England. Like many other returning servicemen, the trauma of war changed them forever.

Our future always contains the horrors of war. Oh! If only the past could teach us how to get along peacefully with our fellow humans. God bless America. We try.

Jo-Ann Cox MacLatchie

At eighty-one, and fifty-seven years into a happy marriage, Jo-Ann remembers the World War II period more vividly than any other. She was in the seventeen-to-twenty-two year old "cusp of life," but now she wishes she could remember her children's childhood as well.

On Saturday, December 6, 1941, I was marching around Boston Common carrying a PEACE sign. I was a seventeen-year-old Emerson College freshman, away from my small Pennsylvania town of Malvern for the first time. I was exhilarated by being on my own in the heart of a big city at last. It was natural that I had connected with a group of fellow student pacifists from the many colleges and universities in the Boston and Cambridge area. Being a birthright Quaker, I had been steeped in the Peace doctrine, and knew that the United States involvement in World War I, which had devastated my parents' generation, had accomplished nothing but to sow the seeds of World War II. Besides, there was this cute guy from MIT who organized the group.

On Sunday, December 7, 1941, I attended Quaker Meeting in Cambridge as usual. Coming back to my dorm on the bus I heard some excited conversation about bombs and Pearl Harbor. I had no idea where Pearl Harbor was, but on entering my building I immediately found out. My sorority sister Keora Kona's home was in Honolulu. Her father was Japanese, her mother was English, and their house was very close to Pearl Harbor. The awful realization dawned on us that Japan had attacked Pearl Harbor while their "negotiators" were sitting with our Secretary of State, Cordell Hull. War became a backdrop to the immediate concern about the status of Keora's parents. Was their house bombed? How could she get through to them?

On Saturday, December 6, 1941, I was marching around Boston Common carrying a PEACE sign.

Jo-Ann in 1946

The next few days were utter chaos. The rumor mill filled the void created by government censorship. It would be many weeks before Keora learned that her parents were all right and their house was not bombed. Casualty and damage information came out piecemeal, and it would be many years before we were told the full enormity of the death and destruction of that day.

On Saturday, December 13, 1941, I was jammed in an auditorium at Boston University with several hundred others of all ages being instructed in how

Many another "just a housewife" found out through such volunteer work how valuable she could be in a paid position.

to identify aircraft—our own and all of the known Japanese and German ones that could possibly be adapted to fly off an aircraft carrier. Sixty-four years later that sounds ridiculous, but after Pearl Harbor, this treacherous, all-powerful enemy had become instantly omnipotent in our minds, and our government leaders encouraged this attitude. With most of our defense weapons sunk, we were woefully unprepared to defend ourselves, let alone take the war to the enemy, which we knew we had to do. The two mighty oceans that had kept wars "over there" suddenly were ponds full of enemy submarines.

This country mobilized overnight, and the war became every man, woman, and child's top priority in life. If we were "the greatest generation" it was because World War II became and stayed personal to each and every one of us. We all collected aluminum cans and bundled newspapers. We all stood in line to give blood, and endured the rationing of gas, meat, tires, etc. Because of the draft, we all had at least one loved one in harm's way, and most of us had ten to a dozen front-line people to pray for every day. We worked impossibly long hours for pay that we had nothing to spend on but war bonds.

My mother was very involved in the war effort despite all her lifetime of working for peace. She volunteered for service with the Pennsylvania Council of Defense, giving thousands of hours to the American Red Cross, for which she was recognized in a document signed by President Roosevelt. She

EMERGENCY SERVICE · AMERICAN RED CROSS

The American National Red Cross

Volunteer Special Services Certificate

This Certifies that Mrs. Jesse Cox has completed the prescribed course for the Canteen Corps conducted by the Southeastern Pennsylvania Chapter of The American National Red Cross.

Issued at Washington, D. C. June 1942

Franklin D Roosevelt, President

Director, Volunteer Special Services

Chairman, Central Committee

Chapter Chairman

Jo-Ann's mother's certificate signed by President Roosevelt

coached a group that put on skits at the local USO, and gave speeches to various organizations on buying bonds and on the conservation of food and energy. She also stitched up blackout curtains for half the houses in Malvern.

Many another "just a housewife" found out through such volunteer work how valuable she could be in a paid position. So it wasn't just Rosie the Riveter who moved women out of the home and into the workforce. These women, like so many other Americans, put the war effort at the top of their priorities, replacing family and household responsibilities.

My father was very active in politics and community affairs in Chester County all his life, so when he was asked to serve on the Draft Board he accepted. He found it necessary to explain to his fellow Quakers that since he knew every pacifist family in that Board's jurisdiction he could validate the claims of all legitimate Conscientious Objectors (COs) and denounce those with false claims. And he was able to help the very few COs who did apply.

Keora's father, who had been a respected business executive before December 11, 1941, was interned somewhere in Hawaii. We all understood the necessity of that action, even Keora. Her mother managed to get back to England, and Keora did not see either parent for five years. She married an Emerson classmate whose family was very wealthy, so she was buffered somewhat from the discrimination shown to anyone of Japanese descent who was not interned.

The cute guy from MIT and thousands of other pacifist students enlisted in their service of choice without waiting to be drafted. I was aware of two men from that group who avoided the draft by declaring themselves COs, but both volunteered as medical corpsmen instead of going to jail. I heard later that one of them died on D-Day.

I did not go back to college for my sophomore year because my parents could not afford it, but I probably would have chosen to stay home even if I had had the option. I wanted to be in the world of work where every job helped the war effort in some way. I had taken an intensive radio course at Emerson, but I had to go to secretarial school to get a job at a Philadelphia radio station. Even then I worked at two other jobs for experience before I landed work at Station WFIL. It was the best of times for a woman in any field, but particularly in radio. I got to perform every job except engineer. Hired to do public relations, publicity, and advertising, I wrote scripts, ran around town with a tape recorder interviewing soldier's families, and had a few on-air stints.

When you heard Ed Murrow's "This is London," you were there.

Jimmy Stewart in Philadelphia to promote "It's a Wonderful Life"

Rudimentary TV was just starting as the war ended. During the war, radio was the medium that allowed us to see the war with our ears. Lowell Thomas and Edward R. Murrow and his "boys" were kings! Yes, you went to the movies at least once a week to be entertained, and always to see the grainy black and white newsreels. But when you heard Ed Murrow's "This is London," you were there. You listened to radio whenever and wherever you could to stay in touch with all the breaking news from the war fronts.

I usually arrived at work at 7:00 a.m., came out

Whenever I see one of our Quaker signs that says, "WAR IS NOT THE ANSWER," I mentally add, "WAR IS STILL THE PROBLEM."

to the lobby at 9:00 a.m. to sign in on the time clock, and then signed out at 5:00 every afternoon, even though I usually took the last train to Malvern about 11:00 p.m. The pay was meager, but I lived off my parents and had no use for money. Besides, I was in radio. I was the person nearest the teletypewriter the day the bells started ringing to announce D-Day and later for the fall of Iwo Jima! I should have been paying the station for those experiences.

Occasionally celebrities stopped by the studio. It was a special day when Jimmy Stewart appeared to promote his new movie "A Wonderful Life." Although this movie is now standard TV fare at Christmas time, it bombed when first released in 1947, probably because none of us wanted to reflect on the past. Perhaps on some level we Americans realized the war had changed our society forever and we knew we were not going back to normal.

Now we are in a new era. In March of 2005 a Marine on duty in Iraq told a reporter, "The Marines are fighting a war, the nation is not." When I see the colored ribbon decals on cars that say, "Support Our Troops," I wonder what that means today. We knew what it meant during World War II. Our news today concerns saving Social Security, oil prices, murder and molestation trials, gay marriage, and, by the way, so many American troops were killed and so many were wounded in Iraq today.

I am still a pacifist. We have fought five wars since the end of World War II, and we have lost every one except the Cold War, where not a shot was fired. We defeated the USSR economically and by encouraging the natural nationalistic desire for freedom and liberty in all the nations they conquered in World War II.

Whenever I see one of our Quaker signs that says, "WAR IS NOT THE ANSWER," I mentally add, "WAR IS STILL THE PROBLEM."

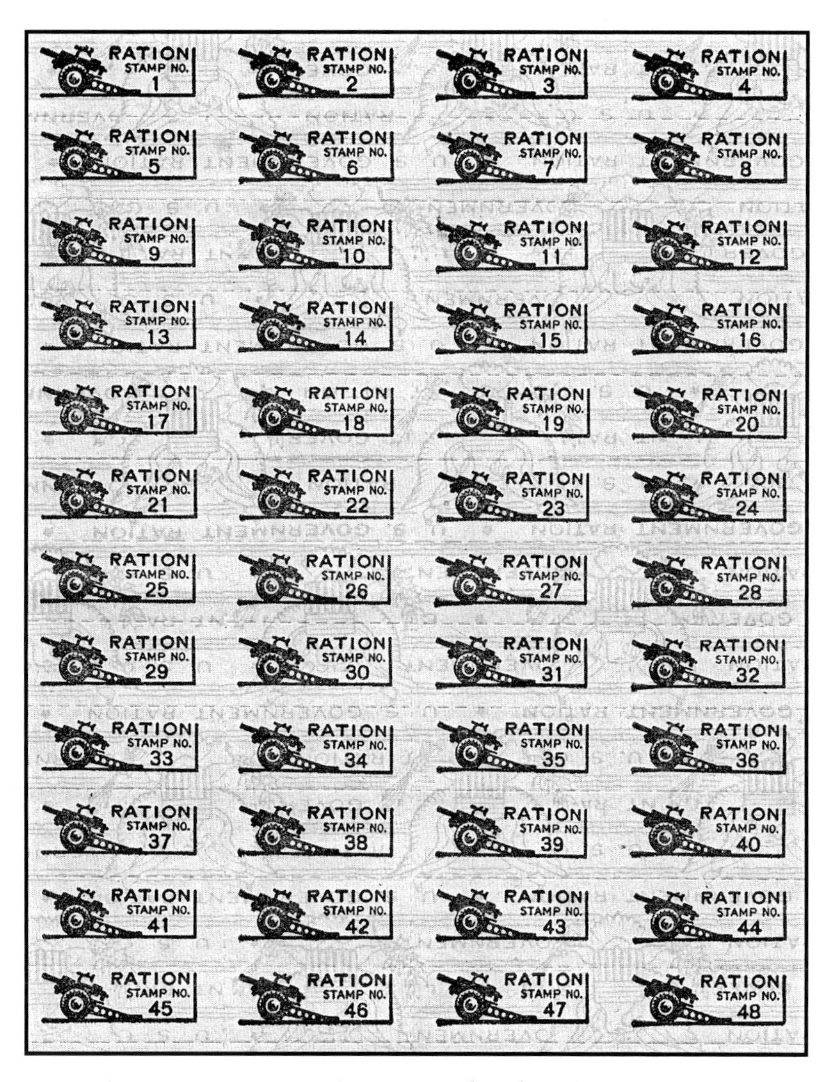

Ration stamp book

Women in uniform

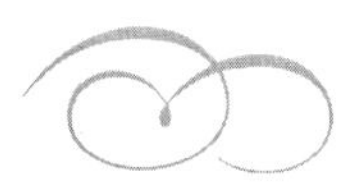

Mary Naomi George Stokes

Naomi grew up in Trumbauersville, Bucks County, Pennsylvania. She and her husband have lived in Chardon, Ohio, since 1956. A married son and two granddaughters live in Georgia. Naomi is an avid reader.

I became a Registered Nurse in 1938, following a three-year course at Presbyterian Hospital in Philadelphia, Pennsylvania. My first job was a twelve-hour night duty shift on the women's surgical ward. In 1939, I temporarily left the hospital for six months to nurse Mother during her illness. She died at home on Sunday evening, January 28, 1940.

I felt somewhat restless when I returned to Presbyterian, spending my time in the surgical ward. Three of my friends were talking about a change. So, when an Army recruiter came to Presbyterian Hospital, we were more than willing to listen to her pitch. It didn't take long for the four of us to accept her challenge. We were inducted into the Army Nurse Corps Reserve January 4, 1941. I was on active duty from then until January 17, 1946.

Some of us had the suspicion that the government had a premonition of the events to follow since they were actively recruiting so many nurses.

Our first assignment was to Fort Belvoir, Virginia, where we joined a group of regular nurses from Washington, D. C. We were a group of forty, living together in a house just for nurses. The patients at Fort Belvoir, nearly all soldiers being trained in the Army Corps of Engineers, were mostly medical and surgical patients. Even at Belvoir, there appeared to be preparations for many wounded. All-wooden hospital units, built something like Quonset huts, were being erected.

Some of us had the suspicion that the government had a premonition of the events to follow since they were actively recruiting so many nurses.

Naomi at home in Trumbauersville

But the war was yet to come, so we had many weekends off. Often we went into Washington (fifteen minutes from Belvoir) with nurse friends who lived there, and we visited many of the public buildings. The Sunday Pearl Harbor was attacked, I was with an Italian nurse at her family's home in Washington.

My sister Ruth had come down to Fort Belvoir the weekend before the war started and we toured the Blue Ridge Mountains of Virginia by bus.

Within a month of the Pearl Harbor attack, volunteers were requested for overseas duty, but we knew not where. By then, two of the nurses who had enlisted with me from Presbyterian Hospital had married and had left the service. (The Army did not want married women.) In January 1942 I was sent to the Panama Canal Zone to a complete hospital unit, 218 General Hospital, stationed at

In January 1942 I was sent to the Panama Canal Zone to a complete hospital unit, 218 General Hospital, stationed at Fort Amador.

Fort Amador. We made the Caribbean trip in three days.

At Fort Amador the patients mainly had malaria. These were men who had gone out into the jungle on expeditions and returned seriously ill. At first they were treated with quinine, but later Atabrin became available and was much more effective. I remember how we covered the men with blanket after blanket in an attempt to lessen their shivering. We also gave them fluids intravenously.

Also at Fort Amador were surgical patients from the paratroop division stationed nearby. They had not yet seen action but suffered from a number of training accidents.

We were on eight-hour duty shifts, and on call if needed. Our food was good and was the same as the military had. We were there almost a year before we received the Army nurses' uniforms—on-duty, white, off-duty, olive drab. We could walk into Panama City—about one mile—or hitch a ride with one of the officers, and eat at the local restaurants. We had occasional drills, but nothing as rigid as the boys had. There were siren alerts when we had to report to a designated area, but Fort Amador was never attacked.

In March 1944, I came back to the U.S. on a troop ship and was sent to McCloskey General Hospital in Temple, Texas, for the duration of the war. Our journey back to the States took two weeks since we stopped in Cuba for several days. We weren't allowed off the ship. I guess they thought it was too dangerous. I'm lucky I was never seasick, but some of the nurses were terribly sick. They were given lemons to suck on and that was about all they did for them.

Fort Belvoir, Virginia

McCloskey was an amputee and paraplegic center plus one ward for military wives and children from Fort Hood, a very large camp. I worked on the amputee ward most of the time, both day and night. One Saturday the ward secretary and I gave a party at her home for patients in wheelchairs. I remember them eating Texas watermelon and roast beef sandwiches. Temple was a one-horse town, but occasionally we dated military men who were ready for discharge from the hospital and the Army.

The men who were amputees seemed to stick together and were supportive of one another. Our work was mostly changing dressings, giving medication, and helping to feed them. Orderlies took care of their other needs, helping them get out of bed and moving them about as needed. The paraplegic men were emotionally more difficult to care for, but we got to know them well since they sometimes stayed at the hospital for many months.

After my Army days were over, I was hired at Crile Veterans Administration Hospital in Parma, Ohio, near Cleve-

Naomi (second from right) with other Army nurses

land. In 1947 I went to college on the GI Bill of Rights and got a B.S. degree in Public Health Nursing at Western Reserve University.

I liked military nursing and think it was easier physically and emotionally than civilian nursing because military patients were generally younger. In the service your roommates and friends were your family. You worked, ate, and slept together just like back home. The camaraderie was great.

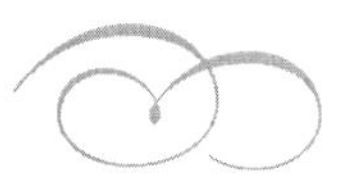

Margaret Theobald Ralston

After her husband's death, Margaret sold their home in Ohio and returned to Honesdale, Pennsylvania. She now resides with her sister, niece and nephew.

Shortly after I graduated from a three-year nursing program at Mercy Hospital in Scranton, Pennsylvania, and against my parents' wishes, I enlisted in the U.S. Army on September 1, 1944. The need for nurses at the front was intense. As a registered nurse and a Second Lieutenant, I was assigned to the 63rd Field Hospital and was sailing out of Boston headed for Scotland on November 10, barely two months after enlisting. It was then on to France and finally to Germany where we learned what war really was.

In February of 1945, in the midst of a raging blizzard, our 63rd Field Hospital servicemen and women set up camp. We were situated at Lovenich, close to where the Ruhr River joins the Rhine and where war was being waged a slight three miles away. In no time, we converted an abandoned farmhouse into a temporary hospital ready to treat seriously injured soldiers.

We could hear the buzz bombs flying overhead, and the casualties started coming in. I had to learn a lot in a hurry.

We could hear the buzz bombs flying overhead, and the casualties started coming in. I was very young and naïve, and had to learn a lot in a hurry. I really grew up quickly. Most of us were shocked at the conditions—we were used to hospitals with plenty of supplies—but we did have some good equipment. We didn't have any extra sheets, and I remember we had to put the poor guys directly from the stretcher onto a cot without sheets. We did what we could with what we had to work with.

Army nurses stationed close to the fighting in Germany

All of us in the medical/surgical unit worked days without sleep as we treated the most critically injured. Our hospital was similar to the unit seen on the TV show M.A.S.H. We treated only non-transportable patients, and worked round the clock many times, as the casualties

Our job was to treat and stabilize the most severely injured, and then evacuate them out as quickly as possible.

kept coming in. Our job was to treat and stabilize the most severely injured, and then evacuate them out as quickly as possible.

At our first set-up in Lovenich, we treated approximately one hundred patients in a few days. Seventy-five of those men survived and were shipped back to the States. Because of their injuries we considered those numbers to be pretty good.

We worked at Lovenich for two weeks and continued to move every three or four weeks as we were needed. Most of the time we set up our emergency hospitals in tents. I was on Temporary Duty (T.D.) with 119 Evacuation Hospital and 41 Evacuation Hospital.

Most of the soldiers we treated suffered from head, chest, and abdominal wounds. It was a real eye opener for a lot of us. It was very difficult to see these young men in pain and we did all we could to treat them and make them comfortable.

The experience was as difficult as it was rewarding. The troops treated us very well. We women were certainly in the minority, yet we were always treated with respect. Everyone understood and appreciated what we were there to do, and it felt very good to be able to help the injured soldiers.

The war in Europe ended in May 1945 and I was back in the States in January 1946. In February I was honorably discharged as First Lieutenant.

The GI Bill gave me the opportunity to pursue further studies. I moved to Cleveland and attended the Francis Payne-Bolton School of Nursing of the Western Reserve University (now Case Western Reserve University), graduating with a BSN degree in nursing. I then worked at the Veterans Administration Hospital in Cleveland for thirty-one years before retiring.

While in Cleveland I met my husband Ted, who was on leave from the Royal Canadian Navy. He had been on active duty since 1939 when World War II began.

As I think back on my years in the Army, I recall how devastating it was to have witnessed some of the young soldiers with such horrendous injuries. The eighteen months I

Margaret (right) in chow line

spent overseas in the Army is a time in my life that I'll never forget. Those months had a major impact on me. How could it not? I was proud to serve my country, and I wanted to go. Although my father didn't want me to enlist, I knew how proud he was of me. My mother later told me that when the guys at the factory where he worked bragged about their sons overseas, he always spoke right up about his daughter, the Army nurse.

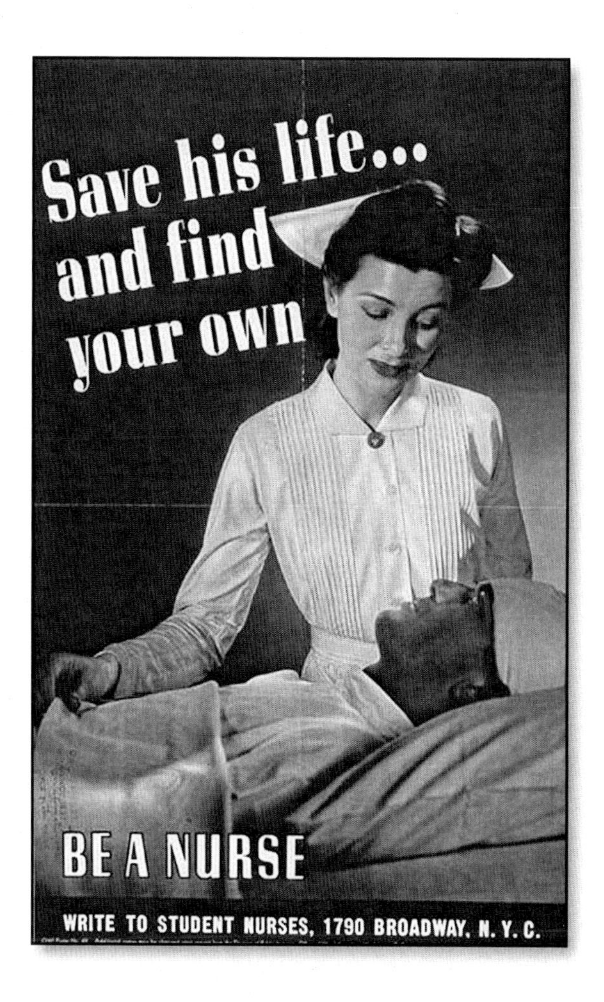

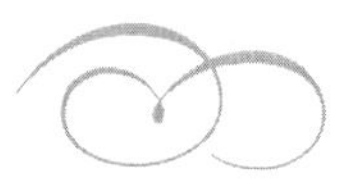

Doris McLean Hays

Doris now lives in a small townhouse where she enjoys reading (mostly nonfiction), doing cryptograms, and visiting friends. She loves to drive, and considers being able to do so a real plus.

I was teaching second grade in Bowie, Maryland, in 1942 after graduating from Beaver College (now Arcadia University) in Montgomery County, Pennsylvania. I liked the children but I didn't like teaching, so I was looking around for something else to do. I enrolled in a secretarial course at Strayer Business School in Washington, D.C. At that time the news broke that women were being accepted for Volunteer Emergency Service by the Navy. I was intrigued and mentioned it to my close friend. She was equally enthusiastic so we agreed to enlist. I signed up on December 19, 1942. She reconsidered and changed her mind. Since there were no billets for officers at that time, I joined up as an enlistee. I made many friends over time and decided to stay where I was.

I was sent to the Navy Training School—boot camp—held at Oklahoma A. & M. University in Stillwater, Oklahoma. I didn't know a soul. We were housed in dormitories, four recruits to a room in bunk beds. Men were also on the base, but had separate quarters. My roommates were from the Bronx, Brooklyn, and from a small town in Massachusetts. The roommate from Brooklyn had competed in "Harvest Moon" dance contests before enlisting and she lived to dance. They held mixers on weekends where she would wear out her partners but never seemed to tire.

We were landlubbers all, but became naval personnel overnight.

Doris, 1943

We were landlubbers all, but became naval personnel overnight. We were jolted awake each morning by the bugler's reveille and the Duty Officer's raucous shout of "Hit the deck!" echoing through the halls. I still enjoy a sense of peace and tranquility whenever I hear taps in the stillness. We were immediately given to know that this was the NAVY and quickly acquired a whole new vocabulary. The walls were bulkheads; the stairs, ladders; the floors, decks; and the bathroom was "the head." The terms became so commonplace that they stuck with you for several weeks after discharge. The obligation to always salute officers was something of a pain (perhaps to them as well), and you often found yourself avoiding them or pretending not to notice them.

Pity you if she found one hair in your hairbrush. Failure to pass inspection could result in your being put on report.

The rumor of an upcoming barracks inspection was enough to give you a case of nerves. I'm sure that the WAVES officer enjoyed intimidating the lowly enlisted. They would arrive wearing the proverbial white gloves. The bunks had to be made up with square corners and covers pulled taut. Pity you if she found one hair in your hairbrush. Failure to pass inspection could result in your being put on report, which involved standing duty, kitchen detail, or some such work.

"Lights out" meant lights out and absolute quiet. One time I had received a package from home, which sat there in the barracks unopened at lights out. We decided to risk the consequences by opening it. It turned out to be my mother's famous orange cake. We looked at each other and asked, "Why not?" We had no utensils so we dug into it with our fingers, polished it off and discarded the evidence. Nothing ever tasted so good.

We must have looked pretty strange to the locals as we marched to classes in our civilian garb for the first week or two. Shortly thereafter we were issued our uniforms: stylish navy and dress whites. The gabardine raincoats with zip-out lining were wonderful and held up well for the whole three years. But the bane of our existence were the cotton lisle stockings with a purplish cast to them and the klunky shoes with fat serviceable heels that we were required to wear. Our skirts were measured from the floor at our fitting to meet the length regulations. Hats were to be worn straight on, and hair was not to rest on our collar.

Then there were the inoculations. We would line up and when we reached the front of the line we passed between two Navy nurses where we received a shot in each arm. I think there was a series of three typhoid shots and two tetanus shots required over time. The typhoid shots caused some of us to feel a little ill for a day or two with a slight fever, but the tetanus shot gave us a very sore arm. Most of us had to have help getting into our jackets because it hurt to lift our arms.

We had to stand watch during the night in shifts. We knew when we were scheduled but it still was a shock to be awakened from a sound sleep by the preceding watch reminding us that it was time to get up and do our shift. When I look back, I realize how ridiculous the whole situation was, since I hardly think anything hazardous to our health was apt to take place in a university dorm in the middle of the night, short of bumping into something while half asleep. But everything was so strict and so "regular Navy" that the fear of God they instilled in us kept us from breaching any regulations. I'm sure the whole Navy routine taught discipline and I can certainly see the necessity for all this today where women are aboard ships and are assigned to dangerous places.

A male sergeant was in charge of the WAVES platoons and responsible for mustering us on the field, preparing us for occasional inspections by a superior officer, teaching us the meaning of the terms "about face," "parade rest," "right oblique," etc., and calling cadence as he marched us to class. We were there from December to March and experienced all kinds of weather, from ice storms in winter—making marching virtually impossible—to wind storms in spring. Oklahoma gave me one gift that I fully appreciated. Being a flat state, its sunrises (and we were always on hand for them) and sunsets were glorious.

In addition to sharpening my secretarial skills as a yeo-

Doris (left end) with other WAVES on a night out.

man, I had to become acquainted with the Navy letter form which was entirely different from civilian business style and required making several color copies for each of the different naval facilities having an interest in the matter at hand. This made correcting typos an arduous task.

Following the completion of our three months of boot camp, we were given three preferences as to where we would like to be assigned. My first choice was the Naval Air Station in Jacksonville, Florida, and I was fortunate to receive that assignment. It didn't take long after arrival to realize that it was a whole new ball game. Barracks inspections were few and far between and much more lenient. Gone were the lisle stockings and more stylish shoes were in vogue. Many items were available to us in the WAVES Ship Store, not the least of which were the nylons that civilians found to be scarce.

We were fed well in the mess hall and received foods that civilians were seldom able to purchase. There was always a complete holiday dinner at Thanksgiving and Christmas and it was at such an occasion that I had my first taste of gooseberry pie.

Fraternization of enlisted personnel with officers was frowned upon but contact through job assignments often prompted mutual interest and led to marriage. Some-

Fraternization of enlisted personnel with officers was frowned upon but contact through job assignments prompted mutual interest.

Since the groom was about to ship out, there was no time to consider protocol. One such wedding had two aviation machinist mates standing there in their coveralls in a hurry to tie the knot.

times, however, it just led to pregnancy, which was cause for discharge and a sad and lonely trip home to family and civilian life. If you did not adhere to a good moral code before you enlisted, you were not likely to establish one in the service.

My first assignment on the base was in the Education Office and had nothing to do with education. I was tasked with writing out ration slips for those going on leave. Whole classes from the Naval Technical Training Center went on leave at the same time and would be lined up down the hallway waiting for their entitlement of three slips—one each for sugar, butter, and coffee. This was to supplement their families' supply of these items. It finally gave me a good case of tendonitis sending me to Sick Bay. The WAVES doctor was unhappy with his assignment and he didn't make any secret of it. He was very cavalier about what he considered to be our petty concerns. He gave me some wintergreen to rub on my arm.

My future at that job struck me as rather dismal, so when I heard there was an opening at the Chaplain's Office, I applied and was hired. At this point, things improved considerably. I was lucky enough to work for a Presbyterian chaplain who was from Norristown, Pennsylvania. He was a reservist and easy to work for. We got along famously. The senior chaplain was a Catholic, regular Navy, and felt the importance of his station. My Catholic roommate worked for him and managed to live through it. Most of my work was writing letters involving personnel stationed there, although sometimes I was asked to stand as a witness to a marriage. Some of the weddings were strange. Since the groom was about to ship out, there was no time to consider protocol. One such wedding had two aviation machinist mates standing there in their coveralls in a hurry to tie the knot. Another time the young bride had come from home to marry her man in the Navy chapel. She brought a gown and walked down the aisle holding a spray of artificial flowers. It was a pretty pathetic sight, but I suppose their happiness was all that mattered.

After about a year on base, we were tired of being surrounded by large numbers of people in the barracks, so three of us rented a house for several weeks on Jacksonville Beach before the summer season began. We were glad to be away from all those regulations and to be able to wear civilian clothes occasionally. I loved hearing the breakers during the night.

During my third year in Florida, I saw that "Join the Navy and See the World" was not about to happen. At one point I considered applying to Japanese Language School at Boulder, Colorado, but I heard it was extremely difficult so I dropped that idea. Later, I had an opportunity to transfer to California by way of Glenview, Illinois. My horizons were expanding and I was all packed and ready to ship out when V-E Day occurred. All transfers were cancelled, except to point of enlistment. Rather than unpack I returned to Washington D.C., and headed for the Chaplain's Office at the Navy Yard in Anacostia, Maryland. Everybody in the reserves was looking to get out, including the chaplain I was assigned to. So I really had nothing to do except wait until I had acquired enough points for discharge, which arrived on December 6, 1945.

The purpose for instituting a women's Navy was to release men from stateside jobs to overseas duty, thereby increasing our naval forces in wartime. I'm not sure that all sailors appreciated this system, but WAVES were trained as yeomen, storekeepers, machinists' mates, control tower operators with responsibility for the safety of planes coming in and taking off, link trainers who taught the men how to fly by instrument, radar technicians, photographers' mates, cryptographers, and many other jobs.

The purpose for instituting a women's Navy was to release men from stateside jobs to overseas duty, thereby increasing our naval forces in wartime.

I enjoyed my Navy experience for the most part and met many wonderful people. It certainly broadened my perspective.

When I returned to civilian life I stayed in Washington working for the United Nations Relief and Rehabilitation Agency (UNRRA), an organization formed to assist war-torn countries to recover from devastation. We entertained doctors from Italy, and engineers and contractors from Russia. They had come to learn from us and then return to serve their own country. I worked as a secretary to a history professor on leave from New York University. He was Norwegian and introduced me to my first smorgasbord. I remained at UNRRA until it closed down, when there was no longer a need for it.

Then I decided to pursue further education under the GI Bill of Rights. I applied to and was accepted at Michigan State College (now Michigan State University). It had a beautiful campus with the Red Cedar River running through it. I took mostly art and music appreciation courses. While there, another ex-WAVE and I re-enlisted in the Reserves and were immediately released to inactive status. We were to get paid whenever we attended meetings. That was in April of 1949. In June of that year I completed two years at the college and returned home to Philadelphia due to my mother's illness. I remained inactive since there was no call for the services of a yeoman in my area. My friend had a storekeeper rating and was called back to active duty, serving for several months.

I was discharged in January of 1954 after having served the Navy for eight years and nine months.

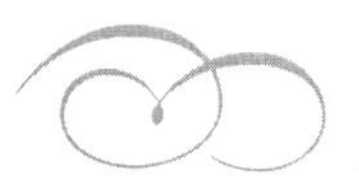

Harriet Green Robinson

Harriet, born in Bridgeport, Connecticut, moved to Los Angeles at age six. She graduated from Hollywood High School and attended University of Southern California and University of California Los Angeles, where she took classes in creative writing.

(Excerpted from** The Gaylord Wacs **by H.G. Robinson)

It was 1943, the year my career as a Wac began. I'd had three weeks of trudging through snow and ice, drilling, freezing, being ordered around and constantly screamed at: "Fall in," "Fall out," "To the right," "To the left," "To the rear march!" I was ready to throw in the towel. My feet hurt and my back ached. The days were horrible, the nights worse. My left arm felt paralyzed from a million injections and my right arm moved like a robot's, continually saluting. I wondered what would happen if I deserted. Would I be shot? At this point I couldn't have cared less. War or no war, I wanted my mother!

Harriet (second from right) and the other Gaylord Wacs

When the Japanese bombed Pearl Harbor, I was living with my charming, live-by-his-wits father and my dreamy, good-times-coming mother in a slightly seedy apartment house in Hollywood, California—one of the many we resided in during my childhood.

Like most Americans, I was unprepared for the way the war would affect my life and my feelings. Food, gasoline, and just about everything was rationed. Most of the eligible men who hadn't yet enlisted were being inducted into military service. Rumors that enemy planes would soon drop bombs on California circulated daily. People became even more confused and frightened when the government rounded up Japanese-Americans and sent them off to internment camps.

Like most Americans, I was unprepared for the way the war would affect my life and my feelings.

My brother Bobby had made it through college, married, and enlisted in the navy. I knew that at twenty-three, I should be doing something better than being a secretary in a law firm, but I wasn't sure what. My acting career was going nowhere. I saw myself as a tragedienne, but my drama coach thought of me strictly as a comedienne.

Going to work by streetcar each day, I saw a poster that fascinated me. It pictured a serious young woman in uniform with the impres-

"This is a woman's war as well as a man's war. Every woman must do her part."

sive words, "This is a woman's war as well as a man's war. Every woman must do her part. One easy way to do your part is to join the Women's Army Auxiliary Corps."

I couldn't get those words out my mind. My love life was hopeless, my acting career was going nowhere, and my self-confidence was at a low point, but my concern and love for my country was still strong. So on December 20, 1942, I joined the Women's Army Auxiliary Corps (WAAC).

At the end of our basic training at Fort Des Moines, Iowa, we expected to be assigned to a specialist school for training as a dental hygienist, an x-ray technician, an optician, or another specialty so that we could take over a man's job and he could go into combat. We chose schools where we thought our talents would be put to best use. Because of my dramatic training, I wondered if I might be sent to the front to help entertain the troops. For me, administrative school was out. But when the rumor spread that we were all being sent to cooks' and bakers' school because the army was desperate for cooks, suddenly administrative school took on new appeal.

Then the word came out that interviews were being held for recruiting duty. I fell in behind the crew and trotted into a room packed with scores of others as desperate as I was. The officer in charge quieted us down. "If you can't drive, take shorthand, type, or do public speaking, get out."

Those of us remaining stayed seated until our names were called. When it was my turn, I was directed to a desk where an officer pointed to a chair. Her first question sent shock waves through my body.

"Do you like the army?" she demanded in a tone which left no doubt about the expected response.

Thank God I had studied dramatics. I responded with every ounce of credibility and enthusiasm I was capable of. "I love it!" I responded. And I was one of two hundred and fifty Waacs chosen to be a recruiter.

Along with four new friends—Helen, Dottie, Fran, and Jo—I was assigned to the Recruiting and Induction District in San Francisco, California. But first we had a layover in Salt Lake City and that's where I met Ralph. My WAAC friends and I met up with a group of Army Air Force officers for a night on the town. Ralph was so nice, a real gentleman, and best of all, he wasn't married. I wondered if I would ever hear from him again.

The WAAC recruiting office in downtown San Francisco was staffed by four WAAC officers, five noncommissioned army officers, three civilian employees, and now five enlisted women.

The army wanted 90,000 more WAAC recruits—18,000 for each of us!—and they provided a small booklet of instructions on how to get them. Much of it turned out to be inspirational messages we had heard in Des Moines. We were the pioneers of a great new experiment and the first impression we conveyed to an applicant was the most important. We were to appear as nice, young, patriotic American girls, which is what we were.

Our superior officer, Lieutenant Faith Chambers, a pretty woman from Atlanta with a southern accent and fluttery hands, was fresh out of Officer Candidate School (OCS), and it was apparent we were the first group of Waacs to report to her.

"All right, girls," she began, "you're in the army now." She proceeded with the long dos-and-don'ts list that we already knew. Uniforms must be worn at all times (except when in our living quarters), light makeup, hair conforming to regulations, and neat nails. We were to convince women of the Bay area that those who joined the WAAC were clean all-American girls, not the tramps the rumors conveyed.

Our first task was to find a place to live, but housing was very tight. We first inquired at the Women's Hotel but that was filled up. As we stood forlornly on the corner of Jones and Geary Streets, Dottie spotted a vacancy sign at the Gaylord Hotel, a typical third-rate old San Francisco hotel, well worn, but with its own charm. The vacancy was a single room, number 110, with two Murphy beds.

"Which two of you is it for?" asked the clerk.

"All five of us," we answered in unison.

Had it been peacetime, she would have told us to get lost. But these were not normal times and it would have been unpatriotic to turn away five members of the service. The clerk summoned the manager who agreed to give us two folding cots and to charge us $80 a month, $16 per person. Perfect!

When Lieutenant Chambers arrived to inspect our quarters, the look on her face was frightening. She could not imagine five women living in these cramped quarters.

When Lieutenant Chambers arrived to inspect our quarters, the look on her face was frightening. She could not imagine five women living in these cramped quarters. But she knew if she didn't approve, she would be responsible for finding us other living arrangements, a challenge she clearly didn't care to face. As she left, she warned us to be ready for impromptu inspections but, as it turned out, this was her one and only inspection.

Fran and Jo were assigned to the administrative office, while Helen, Dottie, and I were involved in active recruitment. Frequently we operated information booths at San Francisco's department stores where we handed out WAAC literature and answered questions. These booths attracted a lot of attention and helped educate the public about the corps. Many people were confused by our uniforms and didn't know who or what we were. One man dropped a fifty-cent piece on top of the leaflets I was handing out. Did he think I was begging or did he think I was collecting for the Salvation Army?

Lieutenant Chambers summoned me to her office to inform me that I had been given a six weeks' assignment to help set up a WAAC recruiting office in San Jose, California. Just before I left her office she informed me I was to give

I didn't know that much about the corps and I definitely couldn't speak to a group of men.

a speech at the San Jose Rotary Club later in the week. I insisted that I couldn't give a speech. I didn't know that much about the corps and I definitely couldn't speak to a group of men. I was not prepared for her next remark, although I guess I should have been.

"You're in the army now, Private, so you learn about the corps. You will speak Tuesday at the Rotary Club in San Jose. This is an order, got it?"

Managing a weak "Yes Ma'am," I saluted and beat a hasty retreat.

I spent the entire weekend preparing for the Rotary. I researched, wrote my outline, memorized my speech and generally felt good about my upcoming assignment. As it turned out, the room was packed and my speech did go very well. Feeling quite confident, I said I would entertain questions.

Someone at the middle table asked how a woman could get out of the corps. I explained the circumstances leading to an honorable discharge including emergencies, death or disability of a family member, or illness. There was one more way—pregnancy, but I couldn't bring myself to say that to a group of men. I had hoped my answers would satisfy them, but then someone asked if there wasn't another way.

"That's right. No other way. Thank you," I said and sat down.

By then they were all laughing, whether at me or with me, but the applause was deafening. I didn't know it at the time, but this was the first of many talks I would give for the army.

Meanwhile, my friend Ralph from my days in Salt Lake City continued to write on a regular basis. His letter of June 11, 1943, indicated he was with a bombardment squadron about to be sent overseas.

On August 30, 1943, we were sitting in Room 110 discussing the latest news. By an act of Congress the WAAC was about to become the WAC—Women's Army Corps. We would all be honorably discharged and had a choice of returning to civilian life or enlisting in the WAC.

We had been in the auxiliary corps for eight months, but now we wouldn't be auxiliaries any longer. We would be entitled to the same pay as the men, receive free medical and dental care and other benefits such as life insurance at army rates, free mailing privileges, government prices at the PX, and special rates at theaters. On August 30, 1943, wearing our winter uniforms, we were sworn into the United States Army at the San Francisco Recruiting and Induction Headquarters.

Meanwhile, the Gaylord Wacs, Room 110, and the Gaylord Bar were almost synonymous. Our fame was spreading and we became the place to be while in San Francisco.

One week the entire officers' complement from the *Grayling*, a submarine in port for repairs, checked into the Gaylord. We soon accepted dates with them, going to the movies, restaurants, and having a good time. Several weeks after we had parted with lots of tears and their promises to return, the *Grayling* was on the evening news. It had been hit by a Japanese mine and sunk. No survivors. The war was coming closer and closer.

In spite of these moments of great sorrow, our life at the hotel was usually fun, but a New Year's Eve party every night could get old pretty fast, even for a buck sergeant in the Women's Army Corps. I was getting restless. About this time my immediate supervisor, Staff Sergeant Graham Kisslingbury, was under a lot of pressure to start a program that would increase enrollment in our district. We, as well as the rest of the nation, were falling behind in our quotas. Thousands more Wacs were needed to fill jobs so the men who now had them could be released for overseas duty.

One afternoon Graham came into the office wearing the self-satisfied smirk we recognized as the sign of a new brainstorm. Usually it meant either more work or more trouble for us, frequently both.

"Congratulations! You lucky guys have been picked to be the charter members of The Flying Team. You'll be traveling on the Silver Bullet (a streamlined army reconnaissance vehicle) to every town, village, and hamlet from Fresno to Crescent City." And thus began another phase in our work. We appeared in various towns at rallies, parades, school assemblies, theaters, and places where there was a crowd. We would put on our little act, singing our little songs and encouraging young women to sign up. Amazing as it sounds, we were a hit and enlistments increased. Nevertheless I was tired of playing the performing soldier. I needed something to do with real meaning, something important.

Recruiting drive

Returning from a Christmas party dedicated to American men and women serving in the armed forces and featuring two badly wounded soldiers who had survived the Bataan death march, my eyes fell upon a poster stating that the army was seeking three hundred Wac privates to volunteer to serve in a company that was being formed for overseas duty. Suddenly my job in San Francisco didn't seem very important. I felt I had to do something more important.

I had had a wonderful year living at the Gaylord and felt good about my work. I had tried to be a good role model for the corps. It wasn't easy taking abuse from parents who didn't want their daughters in the army because we were not nice girls, from men who insulted us, and from that inexhaustible reservoir of suspicion that questioned our purpose in enlisting. Now I was ready for the new challenge of overseas duty.

The first stop in my new life was Fort Ogelthorpe, Georgia, an overseas training camp packed with combat troops caught up in the excitement and anticipation of embarking for Europe or wherever necessary with one thing in mind—victory. But I had forgotten what camp life was like—up at five, lights out at nine, KP duty, marching, drilling, shots, and more shots. When some of us Wacs had the opportunity for a four-hour pass into Chattanooga, we were delighted.

Our first reminder we were in the South were the "white" and "colored" signs on the bus. Even with empty seats in the "white" section, blacks had to move to the back. When this fat, friendly black woman, loaded with parcels, sat down behind us, the bus driver slammed on the brakes and ordered,

Our first reminder we were in the South were the "white" and "colored" signs on the bus. Even with empty seats in the "white" section, blacks had to move to the back.

Two days later, at exactly 5 a.m., the barracks doors opened, the lights went on, and our first sergeant shouted, "Everyone up. This is it."

"Move to the back."

"There's no place back there for her to sit," I protested.

"Mind your own business," he shot back.

"It is my business. Why can't she stay where she is? You make me sick."

"If you don't like it and it insults your northern sensitivity, get off," he growled.

"I don't have to if I don't want to," I responded.

"Okay, Yankees, get off," he said, as he opened the front door. And so we did.

The southerners didn't like the blacks but they didn't like us northerners much either, especially American women who had the audacity to join the army. In their opinion, we had to be tramps. What else?

I was glad when we finally received the news we were moving out. Camp Shanks, about thirty miles from New York City, was our next stop. We all wanted passes to New York, but there was a firm rule that Wacs could receive passes only if we had relatives in town.

I knew I had an uncle, my mother's youngest sibling, living in New York City. He was a successful Wall Street lawyer but my mother had not seen him in years and I was not sure if I had ever seen him. But I found his name in the phone book and called the office. Delighted to hear from his niece, he and my aunt made sure I saw the sights of New York City over the next week or so. But all good things must come to an end and we once again headed out. This time for Newport News, a naval base at Norfolk, Virginia.

Two days later, at exactly 5:00 a.m., the barracks doors opened, the lights went on, and our first sergeant shouted, "Everyone up. This is it." We all cheered. We quickly learned unofficially that we were headed for Naples and should arrive in fourteen days.

Because of the great number of military aboard, not much space was allotted to the Wacs. We were assigned twelve to a stateroom that in peacetime would have accommodated no more than four. With the addition of hammocks, cots, and the bathtub converted into a bed, we all had a place to sleep. Hot water for washing up was available once a day, but some of us who couldn't live without our daily showers could have them as often as we wanted. The only catch was that the water was straight from the ocean—cold and salty.

We spent our days and evenings playing cards, singing and socializing with the military, but still it was boring. When we were issued summer uniforms and equipment, we became somewhat uneasy about our final destination. We were more uneasy when an army colonel and a WAC major entered our stateroom to inform us that we had reached the Strait of Gibraltar and it was possible our ship would be strafed. We were to be prepared to abandon ship.

I continued to receive regular letters from Ralph. In a letter from England dated February 10, 1944, he mentioned having been decorated for exceptionally meritorious achievement during five separate bomber combat missions over Germany. He always included plans for when we would see each other after the war.

Our ship landed in Naples June 3, 1944, three days before D-Day. As the army trucks drove us through Naples, we were startled by our reception. Mobs of people had lined the streets shouting, "Viva Americana," to the Americans who had helped save them.

Our food was good but we had to eat outdoors and as soon as we appeared so did the children, begging for food. We gave them all that we had but it was heart rending. The hungry children and the sight of bombed buildings and much destruction made me realize once again that my little troubles in life weren't all that important. If I hadn't come of age before, I had now.

It wasn't long before the news of Eisenhower's victory in France spread and we were sure the war would be over soon. But in the days to come we began to realize it was far from over.

When we heard the Red Cross was asking for blood donors we went to the hospital. The officer in charge said they were short-handed because of the huge number of soldiers wounded in the invasion and he wondered if we could help. Our commanding officer granted the request.

If I thought the sight of Naples was horrible, nothing had prepared me for the horror we encountered at the hospital. Hundreds of men who had survived the slaughter of D-Day were being brought in on stretchers. Some had lost a leg, some an arm, some both. The nurses were overloaded so we helped out where we could—talking with the soldiers, writing letters for them, being present when they regained consciousness following surgery. This was another moment when I was glad I had joined the army and could help in some way, no matter how small.

Harriet (left), roommate, and Egyptian boy in Cairo, Egypt

And then the word came: "Pack!"

It was late afternoon when we boarded the Polish ship *Batory*, carrying English troops. The meals were wonderful and afternoon tea brought us cookies, small tea sandwiches, and all sorts of delicacies. It was a great experience being on the ship with the English. We were impressed with their love for their country, and when they sang, "There'll Always Be an England," we realized the Germans could continue bombing them every night, but could never defeat them.

And then we received the announcement, "You are reaching your destination tomorrow. We are landing in Alexandria, Egypt. You are now assigned to the United States Army Forces in the Middle East (USAFME). Headquarters are in Cairo and you will be at Camp Huckstep for a few weeks, and then you will be given a permanent assignment.

I was fortunate to be assigned as secretary to a high-ranking officer, something I had always hoped for. The colonel really didn't need a sec-

We were informed that we were absolutely forbidden to associate with Farouk, Egypt's fat, twenty-four year old king.

retary since he already had a major, a captain, first and second lieutenants, several enlisted men, and now a bunch of Wacs. My major responsibility was getting coffee for him and other headquarters staff in the morning, and Cokes for them in the afternoon. It was depressing.

Along with all the other regulations we encountered, a new one appeared on the bulletin board. We were informed that we were absolutely forbidden to associate with Farouk, Egypt's fat, twenty-four year old king. We saw him often in the local bars and restaurants, accompanied by bodyguards and gorgeous women in sparkling gowns and jewels. Occasionally, the King would send one of his henchmen to our table and ask us to join him, but we had to refuse.

Mail call was the highlight of the day, but on one particular day, my friend was acting strange when the mail arrived. She handed me two letters but held back on one. It was my last letter to Ralph. I saw the words inscribed, "Return to sender. Addressee reported missing in action."

I later learned that Ralph's plane had gone down somewhere over Germany. The plane and its entire crew were lost. Even though I wasn't sure Ralph and I would ever meet up with one another again, there was an ache in my heart.

Sitting in the airport café en route to the island of Cyprus for a week's furlough, I learned from a clipping in the *Stars and Stripes* that Franklin Delano Roosevelt had died April 12 at Warm Springs, Georgia. Harry Truman was our new president. We were all shattered. Most of us had never known a president other than Roosevelt and we remembered the Great Depression when there wasn't enough food to go around and when our mothers shared food with hungry men who begged for food on our doorsteps.

After a pleasant week on Cyprus riding bicycles, taking hikes, partying on the beach, and swimming in the Mediterranean, we arrived back in Cairo to learn that the Italian dictator, Benito Mussolini, had been executed. Later that month, Adolph Hitler committed suicide as the Russians were about to enter Berlin. On May 8, 1945, President Truman declared V-E Day, the end of the war in Europe. Later that summer, August 15, 1945, came V-J Day, finally putting an end to the killing.

Within a few months I was homeward bound. Upon arriving in Newport News, Virginia—to a big reception with steak and all the ice cream we could eat—we were assigned to temporary quarters. Although it was early in the day, I was exhausted and went to my room and flopped down on my bunk. Suddenly two WAC officers walked in and I pulled myself up to attention.

"Oh no, don't get up. Is there anything we can do for you?" they inquired.

I was too astonished to say anything, and then it dawned on me. I was an overseas veteran and they were impressed.

When I sat back down, I noticed two other Wacs in the room. We smiled and then I looked again. Was I seeing things? They were Negro Wacs and we were sleeping in the same room and eating at the same table. I soon learned that President Truman had set the wheels in motion to ban racial discrimination in the armed forces. Maybe it's going to be a kinder world after all, I thought.

In October, 1945, I was back in Des Moines where my

army career had begun thirty-four months previously. I received my Honorable Discharge and a certificate listing my qualifications: "Public relations man, types, answers phone." I always felt the army didn't appreciate my talents, but I wished they could get one thing straight for the record—I'm a woman.

I returned home to Los Angeles. My brother was out of the navy and home with his family. My parents were relieved that their children had returned safely from the war and I was happy to be back home to just relax for a time.

In February of 1946 the Gaylord Wacs all came together for a marvelous reunion weekend in San Francisco. We talked and ate and talked and ate some more as we caught up on each other's lives. We vowed to keep in touch with one another, but we knew it would never be the same again. We could not go back to our former lives but we would never forget the time that five WAC recruiters had lived together, in a single room. We had served our country well.

Women at work

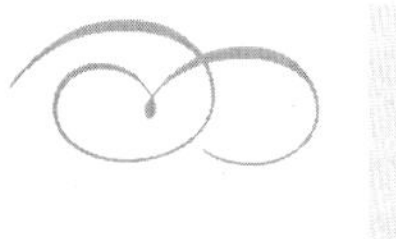

Irene Chipman Bottenfield Hewitt

Irene lives in Warrington, Pennsylvania, with her daughter and son-in-law. She enjoys activities at the Naval Air Station in Willow Grove, Pennsylvania, ballroom dancing, and reading.

On December 7, 1941, we were visiting an uncle in Metuchen, New Jersey. After a midday dinner, my brother and I left the adults to go to the soda fountain at the local drugstore. While there, we heard on the radio that Pearl Harbor had been attacked. We ran home to tell the others.

In 1942, I graduated from Drexel University after majoring in home economics. Since most of the men in our class were going off to war, it was a good time for women graduates to find employment in industry. My friend Barbara and I quickly found jobs with the Hercules Powder Company at their Experimental Station in Newark, Delaware. Their main office was in Wilmington.

I was raised in Ridley Park, Pennsylvania, and my family was still living there in 1942. Barbara and I shared an apartment in the YWCA in Wilmington and rode the bus to work every morning. We had free passes because we were in defense work.

I worked the day shift in the analytical department of the Experimental Station, calibrating glassware to make sure the markings were accurate. New equipment had been introduced and my job was to insure that these new bottles had the exact number of liters.

In December of 1943, on my birthday, the *New York Times* displayed my photo as part of its "Women in Industry" series. The accompanying article mentioned that I was a home economics graduate with a lot of chemistry studies.

My friend Barbara worked in the chemistry lab on a product that would eventually become a detergent for washing clothes. Until then there were no detergents. Instead we used packaged soap flakes or soap chips.

My father was a self-trained lighting engineer working

THE NEW YORK TIMES, SUNDAY, DECEMBER 6, 1942. WOMEN'S CLUBS

THE WAR WIDENS HORIZONS FOR WOMEN IN LABORATORY AND FACTORY

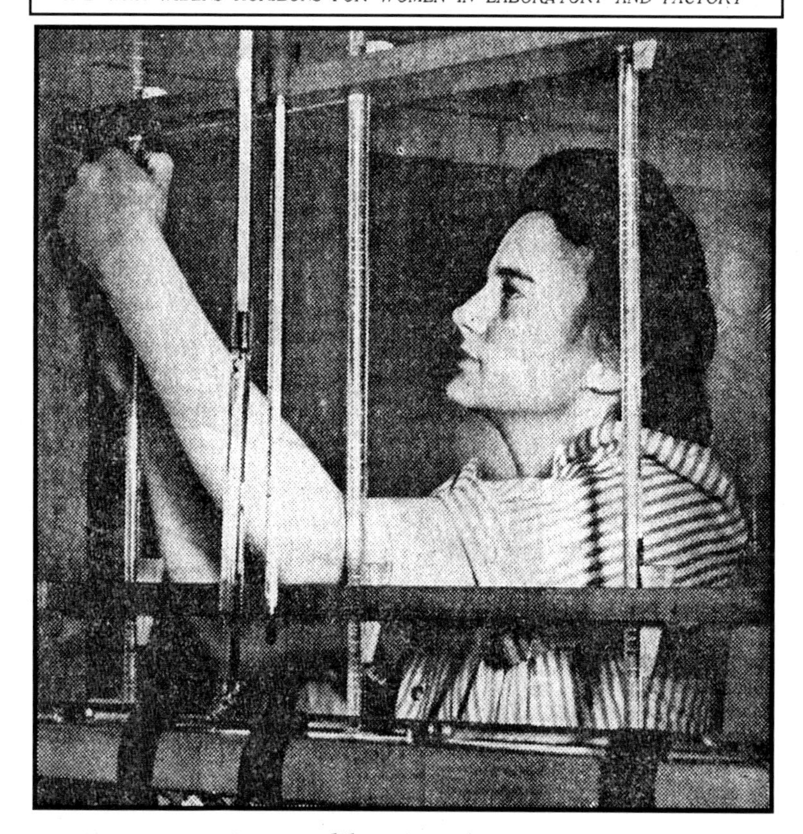

Irene calibrating glassware

On June 6, 1944, I was lying in bed when I heard the singsong voice of the paper boy announcing the invasion of Europe.

for General Electric in Philadelphia. The company sent him to work at the Norfolk Shipyard, so our family moved to Richmond, Virginia. At one point, my father designed the lighting for the ocean liner SS *United States*. I believe it transported troops back then.

After moving to Richmond, I found employment with the Virginia Electric and Power Company (VEPC). Electricity for home use, other than lighting, was just beginning to come into fashion. My job was to answer questions and give demonstrations to women, teaching them how to use electric ranges. Until then, gas stoves had been the norm.

Part of my job was to give cooking lessons to the Girl Scouts. We made a variety of baked goods using the new electric range. This was before aluminum foil was a common kitchen commodity, but the Reynolds Company had given samples of the foil to the VEPC for experimental use. Our Girl Scouts made fruitcakes and wrapped them in aluminum foil to give to the company executives. Several years later, the product became available to the general public.

To relieve the tedium at work and also bring a little fun into our lives, we had a fashion show. I wore a two-piece bathing suit, rather daring back then.

On June 6, 1944, I was lying in bed when I heard the singsong voice of the paper boy announcing the invasion of Europe. I ran downstairs, turned on the radio, and ran out for a paper.

In Richmond, Mother and I were hostesses at the USO Canteen. Mother would often invite servicemen home for dinner. One of the fellows, from Philadelphia, gave me a traveling kit with various makeup accessories. I still have it.

Rationing woes

Back in college a number of us female students attended dances at various military installations. We were taken by bus to Aberdeen Proving Grounds in Maryland and to Fort Dix and Fort Monmouth in New Jersey. There we danced and sang with the servicemen.

On September 13, 1944, I gave my first pint of blood at the Veterans Hospital in Richmond. Walking home at 9:00 p.m., I heard footsteps behind me. I thought it was a man hurrying home from work on this rainy night but as I looked out the corner of my eye, I saw a sailor's white uniform under his raincoat. Then I realized there were two of them approaching me. I tried to hold tight to my pocketbook but they overpowered me and took it. I went to a nearby house and asked if I could report the robbery to the police, but they said they were having a party. So I went across the street. The next day, a worker for the Atlantic Trucking Company found the scattered contents—my shoe ration coupon, a pen with my name engraved on it, a brown leather bag, my glasses and a Revlon lipstick, which was my only lipstick. The day after the robbery, I had to go to work without lipstick.

We had coupons for butter, meat, sugar, cigarettes (which didn't bother me), shoes, and gas. We took our coupons when we went to the store. I can still see my mother pulling my brother's little wagon to the store to bring the groceries home. And silk stockings were at a premium, so we used leg makeup. We applied this brown liquid to our legs to make it look like we were wearing stockings. You had to do it carefully so it didn't streak, or as one of the men said, "It looks like you had an accident." Nylon stockings had been available very briefly, but were taken off the market to be used for parachutes and other wartime necessities.

We had two containers for the trash. Back then, we had to take off both ends of tin cans and then step on the can to smash it as flat as we could. We also saved bacon fat and hardened it in the refrigerator. I think it was used for ammunition. After it was hardened, we would take it to the butcher. Our butcher had a sign in his window, "Don't bring your fat cans in here on Saturday."

> ***Our butcher had a sign in his window, "Don't bring your fat cans in here on Saturday."***

Every day at noon, we listened to Kate Smith sing "God Bless America." And we listened to an English woman, Gracie Fields. She would hold that one note so long. Some of my favorite songs were "Slow Boat to China," "Tangerine," "Yours," and "Isle of Capri."

Following V-E Day on May 8, 1945, our family moved back to the Philadelphia area. I went to work for the Philadelphia Electric Company doing much the same customer service tasks that I had done in Virginia. But now I was to put forth a new image. We had to wear hats to work and some of the women were even sent home if their lipstick was smeared. It was the new era of professional women and we were expected to look the part.

When the war in Japan ended on August 14, 1945, I was living on the eighteenth floor of the YWCA in Philadelphia. When I heard the news, I ran out on the balcony, screaming with joy as I joined with the rest of the city in celebrating peace—peace that had been a long time in coming.

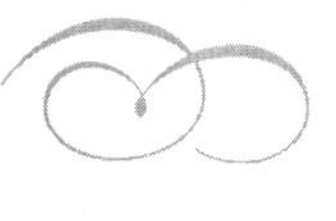

Elinor May Driscoll Murphy

In 1942, Elinor was a young girl filled with patriotism. Today, she is blessed with six children, eighteen grandchildren, and four great-grandchildren. She hopes she has instilled patriotic fervor in them.

The town of Hingham, Massachusetts, was incorporated in the year 1635. Many of its citizens remained loyal to the crown. Others claimed connections to voyagers on the Mayflower.

Hingham, thirty miles south of Boston and twenty miles north of Plymouth, prospered and grew. It was essentially a coastal town, with shipbuilding, dairy farming, and trading being the primary industries.

Hingham boasts the oldest church in continuous use in America: the Unitarian church, Old Ship Church. Its architecture is an upside down ship, the keel being its roof. There is also a fascinating graveyard dating back to 1635, its gravestones featuring poems about the deceased, many of them children. As youngsters, we frequently picnicked in the graveyard three hundred years later.

Elinor (standing center) at USO

During John Adams's presidency, there were rumors of making Hingham a summer White House. The main street was widened and two frontage roads were created on either side to allow the presidential entourage to drive into town unimpeded. But the summer White House never materialized.

"Help Wanted" signs sported the words, "No Irish Need Apply."

This proper Puritan society thrived for 230 years, until the Irish famine drove millions of Irish to American shores. In 1865 my grandfather, Peter Driscoll, landed in the port of Boston. Back when he arrived the Irish were treated very poorly. They had to step in the gutter when English people walked by. "Help Wanted" signs sported the words, "No Irish Need Apply." Despite my grandfather's position as schoolmaster in Ireland, no such employment was offered in this new land which was raging with bigotry. He found work selling Bibles door to door, carrying two heavy Bibles hanging from a rope around his neck. He married, fathered two sons, and died at age forty-two of pneumonia.

During the intervening years, a few Ital-

The Japanese attack on Pearl Harbor, where I lost a cousin on the ship Arizona, galvanized America and Hingham into action against a common enemy.

ian immigrants arrived to seek their fortune in a hostile place, but they were scorned and clustered to the peripheral areas of the town, like Kilby Street in North Hingham. Other than being employed as gardeners for the wealthy landowners, they were not absorbed into the general populace. From their own little gardens they pooled what they had produced and once a week they drove a horse and wagon through the streets of Hingham selling fresh fruits and vegetables.

One Russian family and three Finnish families lived in a wooded area on the outskirts of town. The Russian insisted he was part of the nobility who had escaped the overthrow of the Czar. Neither he nor the Finns mingled much with the regular townsfolk, although the children attended school.

Fast forward to December 7, 1941. The Japanese attack on Pearl Harbor, where I lost a cousin on the ship Arizona, galvanized America and Hingham into action against a common enemy. Young men by the hundreds joined the Army, the Navy, the Marines and the newly created Army Air Corps.

In 1909, a naval ammunition depot had been established in Hingham. During the years before the war, the depot and the presence of a contingent of Marines were taken for granted by the townspeople. However, after the onset of the war the depot supplied the North Atlantic Fleet with torpedoes, ammunition, and mines.

But the big change in Hingham occurred in 1942 with the construction of the longest steel mill in the world. The Bethlehem-Hingham Shipyard employed hundreds of local people. During its first few years, the shipyard produced DE's (Destroyer Escorts) for the British Navy, and later for the U.S. Navy. Then in 1944, the shipyard switched to building LST's (Landing Ship Tanks) and LSI's (Landing Ship Infantry), which ultimately were used in the D-Day invasion.

The distaff side of sleepy Hingham was called into service also. Our mothers made bandages and other knitted articles, while some of us learned to identify enemy aircraft.

Many of the younger women were called upon to entertain our troops in a facility known as a USO meeting place. A fabulous home in the center of Hingham in the upscale part of town, was purchased to serve as the USO center. At the USO, we played the piano, sang, danced, and helped make the troops forget the reality that they soon would be heading off to war. Some of the girls went to the USO only on the nights the officers would be on hand, but others of us were there for anyone in uniform. We entertained French sailors (amorous), British sailors (earthy), and we were particularly fond of the reserve soldiers from the Worcester, Massachusetts, area.

Popular music of the time included "Don't Sit Under the Apple Tree," sung by the Andrews sisters, "The White Cliffs of Dover," sung by Gracie Fields," and other favorites including "As Time Goes By," "We'll Meet Again," "I'll Be Home for Christmas," and "Lili Marlene."

My father was concerned about my safety, since I sometimes walked a couple miles to our home late at night after the dances. He made me a cudgel—a heavy weight attached to a piece of clothesline wrapped around my wrist like a bracelet. If I heard anyone suspicious approach me, I was to wallop him with this weight.

By this time, the government had established Camp Hingham in the southern part of town, about five miles out in the woods. It was a staging ground for Army reservists, the last stop before being shipped out. We later learned with great sadness that the lovely boys we danced with from Worcester were totally wiped out on D-Day. They were the first wave of soldiers to go ashore.

Bethlehem-Hingham Shipyard

Upon graduation from high school, I was awarded a year's scholarship to attend Wyndham School, a finishing school for girls. It was in an old brownstone on Marlboro Street in the ritzy Back Bay part of Boston. There I learned good manners, proper speech, and how to behave at tea dances. I also sharpened my secretarial skills.

Soon I was employed at Hingham Shipyard as a secretary to the head of the Accounting Department. I was his personal secretary, taking dictation in shorthand and typing his letters. The department was a huge open room. In order to facilitate communication, my boss had installed a blue light which he activated by a button when he wanted me. One day, a wag (joker) substituted a red light for my blue light. Being an innocent of the forties, the meaning escaped me. An older, wiser co-worker alerted me. I felt humiliated. I was one of the younger workers. I recall the woman who sat next to me telling me that she had lost her entire family—husband and children—in the influenza epidemic of 1917-18.

On a lighter note, I was invited by a British officer to a christening of an LST. Innocence rampantly marching again, I loved the champagne cocktail with the warm beer chaser. Never mind that since my parents were teetotalers I had never had an alcoholic drink. My last memory was of a proper British driver depositing me in the kitchen of my parents' home.

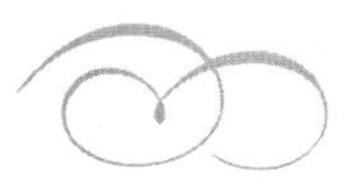

Elsie Scarborough Hewitt

Elsie and her husband live in Havertown, Pennsylvania. They have two daughters and four grandchildren. Elsie was a school secretary in the Havertown Township School District for twenty-four years.

Since our nineteen-year-old mother died when we were born, my twin sister Eleanor and I grew up with our paternal grandparents on Ocracoke Island, on the Outer Banks of North Carolina. My father was in the Army Corps of Engineers working on the dredges and away from home frequently. He began working on the dredges at the age of sixteen and as time went by he was made Captain of his boat, the *Gillespie*, and finally became Superintendent of all the dredging on the Delaware River and Bay, the Chesapeake Bay, and the connecting canal. He had offices in New Castle, Delaware, and Philadelphia. For awhile we lived in Salem County, New Jersey, but later moved to Chester, Pennsylvania.

Back when we lived on Ocracoke, only a few hundred people resided there and practically all the men were fishermen. Since we were completely surrounded by water, boats were the major means of transportation and the only way to go to the mainland for food and supplies. My grandfather was a builder and built most of the houses and many of the boats on the island. He also constructed the first motel.

Occasionally small boats attached to ships washed up on the shores of the Outer Banks and, sometimes, even bodies washed up.

Elsie modeling for American Viscose magazine

After we moved away, we kept in regular contact with friends on the island. Shortly after Hitler declared war on the United States in December of 1941, we heard that German submarines were traveling freely just off American beaches, sinking ships up and down the coast. Occasionally small boats attached to ships washed up on the shores of the Outer Banks and, sometimes, even bodies. Residents could see ships burning at sea and were saddened by the realization that many boys were burning up with them. It was a sad time.

There was always a Coast Guard Station on the island for as long as I could remember. The fellows had to walk through our property whenever they left the station, and some of the girls on the island

The Navy told my grandfather that he would have to leave his home. They even placed dynamite on my friend's porch.

married them and moved away. There weren't many boys on the island since most of them left to find work up north. I recall that Daddy hired a few of them to work on the dredges.

In 1940, something very upsetting occurred. The Navy told my grandfather that he would have to leave his home since they needed it to establish a naval base there. The Navy did the same to my grandfather's brother Charlie who lived next door, and to a good friend who lived in a third house. Each was offered a pittance for what the houses were worth and they were told if they refused their houses would be dynamited.

Now my grandfather had built his home and had lived in it with my grandmother since 1885. His father had lived on the property before him. It would not be easy to find another house as houses usually became available only when someone moved away or died. It was decided that our family, including my grandfather, would move to Chester to be closer to my father's work.

Uncle Charlie did find a home on Ocracoke but our friend's family had nowhere to go. They wanted to stay in their home, but the Navy was adamant. They even placed dynamite on my friend's porch. They still had no place to go, but out of fear, they left their house and lived in a tiny shack without running water or utilities until something became available.

The area close to our home became a naval training camp and the homes were turned into quarters for the officers. When the war was over, the houses were all torn down. Shortly thereafter the training camp was closed without a trace of its ever having been there, and a new Coast Guard Station has been built.

Ocracoke is no longer just a fishing village but has become a prime spot for vacationers. Tourism is now its number one industry.

I was still in high school when World War II broke out, living in Chester. I graduated from Chester High School in 1942 and went to work for the American Viscose Company in Marcus Hook, Pennsylvania, where they were making nylon cord for parachutes and tires. I was a bookkeeper in the accounting department. Every payday I was able to purchase enough rayon stockings for my sister, my stepmother, and myself.

Former Coast Guard station at Ocracoke Island, N. C.

I was chosen to model a dress made of printed rayon for *Crown Rayon News*, an in-house magazine showing what was actually made at Viscose. I remember a photographer coming to our house to take pictures of me by the stairs. Then we went to Chester Park where he took more pictures by the falls.

We were all involved in the war effort in some way. I took a First Aid course sponsored by the American Red Cross and was given a cap and an apron, but I was never called to serve. We had blackouts when we all had to stay indoors. I recall one night when the air raid warden told my boyfriend there would be a double blackout that night. Usually, George had to leave our house at eleven o'clock, but that night we were still in a blackout until midnight. My mother was quite upset that George had to stay past eleven o'clock.

George and I were visiting one of my favorite teachers when a Western Union man came to the door with a telegram. It announced that her son, her only child, had been killed in the Battle of the Bulge. When she received the news, she ran into the kitchen and refused to see anyone. We were worried lest she would turn on the gas and commit suicide. It was a terrible night. She had lived for this boy. It wasn't long before she moved to California to be near a sister and she never returned to the East Coast.

As happy as we all were to see the end of the war, for many the heartache of war remained forever.

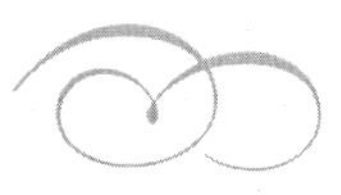

Lillian Wismer Sweet

Lillian was born in Plumstead Township, Pennsylvania. She has lived her entire life in the central part of Bucks County. At the age of ninety-six, Lillian continues to have a lively mind.

When the war broke out I was living in New Britain, Pennsylvania, working at Chalfont Hosiery Mill. I was a "pairer," matching up two stockings after they came from the "boarder," the person who put a board in the nylon stockings to shape them. He put them in piles of sixes, in different lengths. Then I would match them up. We were paid for the number of pieces we did, and you can't live on what they pay for piecework.

Then came the war, and workers were needed at Johnsville, Pennsylvania, at the Brewster Aircraft Plant. I worked eight-to-five, six days a week. It was a large plant and I lost weight with all the walking I did. Here they paid by the hour.

My first job was to rivet little metal pieces to each part of the aircraft. I was so fast I got the nickname of "Shotgun Lil." Rosie the Riveter got all the publicity but I did the same thing she was doing. These little metal pieces had an identification number on them for use when assembling the plane.

Lillian (right), sister Helen, and Bob

It was discovered that some planes had been assembled without the proper metal pieces, so another woman and I were sent across the street to a building that housed the assembled planes. We didn't know it at the time, but the planes had already been fueled. After we finished our work and had returned to our own building, we were told that we could have been blown to pieces using electrical equipment near fuel. Well, I'm still here and I'm ninety-six years old.

After we finished our work and had returned to our own building, we were told that we could have been blown to pieces.

After awhile I was promoted to B Mechanic. No, I didn't get a raise. My job was to insert the wheels into the back end of the plane after it had been assembled. I would put my hand up into the space, find the hole where I would put the screw to hold the wheel in place. I did a lot of crawling around so I wore my husband's pants. The planes we worked on were for the Army. The Navy planes were in a different building.

After the plane was built, it would be tested, then brought back to the plant where the wings were removed and all the parts were boxed in a long container the size of a plane. They were

The boxes had holes drilled in them to make sure they would sink to the bottom of the sea, in case the ship came under enemy fire.

then shipped by boat to England where they were reassembled. The boxes had holes drilled in them to make sure they would sink to the bottom of the sea, in case the ship came under enemy fire.

I had another job at the plant, placing the long fuel pipes inside the fuselage. Occasionally I found two people inside the plane doing things they shouldn't be doing. Our plant got the nickname of "Bucks County Play House."

We had morning and afternoon breaks and a lunch break. I ate my main meal of the day in the plant cafeteria. I never missed a day, even in the worst snowstorms. I'd get up early to go out and put clamp-ons on my tires. They don't allow them anymore because they tear up the road, but I never missed a day.

I had five other riders I picked up at a certain location in Doylestown, Pennsylvania, at a given time. If anyone was late, we just went along without them. Of course, we might wait a minute or so, but no longer. My riders gave me their gas rations in return for the ride.

Meanwhile, my husband, Bob, was in the Navy. We were married in 1929. He wasn't called up, but he enlisted before being drafted into the Army. He said he didn't want to slosh around in the mud. He was sent to Great Lakes Naval Station to be trained as a gunner. He was shipped back east to North Beach, Maryland, where he had target practice, shooting streamers attached to old airplanes. He came home every other weekend and I would drive to Philadelphia, Pennsylva-

nia, to pick him up.

The owner of the gas station told me I would always be able to get gas for my serviceman husband. I had a little trouble with the owner of the meat store, however. I had ordered a nice roast beef for one of the weekends Bob would be home. When I arrived to pick it up, he told me he had sold it to someone else. I was mad.

After the war, Bob was shipped to Hawaii for a short while. Meanwhile, I had saved enough money to pay off the mortgage on our house. I saved every bit of money I could from my salary and from the $50 the government sent me every month. And I went to church every Sunday.

I carried with me a short story titled "Deck of Cards." It's about a soldier who found all he needed to know about religion in a deck of cards. I've carried it in my wallet over sixty years.

When the war ended, we were all laid off from the aircraft plant. I went back to piecework, this time at the Fretz Pants Factory where they had made pants for the Army during the war. Now they were making men's trousers for civilians.

It wasn't long before Bob was home for good, and we were able to resume normal lives.

A Deck of Cards

During the war, a group of soldiers arrived at a small village in France after a long march. The chaplain read a prayer and asked all the men who had Bibles to open them. One of the soldiers brought out a deck of cards. He was arrested and taken to the commanding officer.

"Sir", he said, "I have neither Bible or prayer book, but I hope I can satisfy you with the purity of my intentions.

"You see, sir, when I look at the ace it reminds me that there is only one God. When I look at the duce it tells me the Bible is divided into two parts, the Old and the New Testament. The three represents the Father, the Son and the Holy Ghost.

"The four calls to mind the four evangelists, Matthew, Mark, Luke and John. The five reminds me of the five wise virgins, the six that in six days the Lord made heaven and earth, and the seven that He rested on the seventh day.

"The eight is the eight righteous persons God saved when He destroyed the earth by flood — Noah, his wife and their three sons and their wives. When I look at the nine I think of the lepers our Savior cleansed and nine of them did not thank Him.

"The 10 reminds me of the Ten Commandments.

"When I look at the king I think of our Lord. The queen reminds me of the Virgin Mary. When I see the jack I think of the devil.

"When I count the spots on the cards I find 365, the days in the year. There 52 cards in the deck, the 52 weeks in a year. There are four suits, the four weeks in a month. There are 13 tricks, the 13 weeks in a quarter. There are 12 picture cards, the 12 months in a year.

"So you see, sir, my deck of cards serves as a Bible, almanac and prayer book."

Newspaper Enterprise Association

Lillian's deck of cards

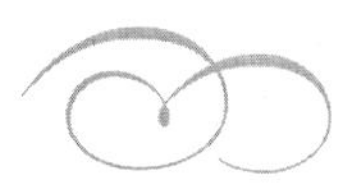

Alverta Carver Clime

Alverta is soloist with the Pennridge Merrymakers Orchestra, and also sings with The Joyful Singers and the Senior Citizens Chorus, all in Bucks County, Pennsylvania.

It is hard to imagine today that there was such a store as Clymer's where they sold just about anything . I remember going to the basement to pump molasses out of a barrel.

After graduating from Doylestown High School in 1932, I went to work in Smith's Dairy at Decatur and Wood Streets, just up from Union Street in Doylestown. A woman from nearby Chalfont who had a candy shop, taught some of us girls how to coat candy with chocolate. We would dip vanilla and chocolate butter creams into a chocolate coating. If the butter cream was vanilla, we marked it by running a string through the chocolate; if the butter cream was chocolate, we marked it with our finger.

I met my future husband, Henry Clime, at the Grange Hall in Buckingham, where they held dances every Friday night, usually with a very good dance orchestra. Five of us girls who had been coating chocolate wanted to go to one of the dances, so the owner of the candy shop said she would chaperone us. Imagine needing a chaperone!

At any rate, someone introduced Henry and me. He seemed to like dancing with me and asked me for a date the next night. It was also in Buckingham, but this time it was at the Paxafom, which had a wonderful dance floor. It's now Brown Brothers Auction.

Alverta in her Red Cross uniform

About this time I went to work at Clymer's Department Store in Doylestown. I had wanted a bookkeeping job but none was available, so I was assigned to various departments throughout the store. It is hard to imagine today that there was such a store as Clymer's where they sold just about anything from groceries to toys to refrigerators to heaters. I remember going to the basement to pump molasses out of a barrel.

As you entered the store there was a long table several feet long and about four feet wide covered with things for sale, and everything on the table cost three cents. I still have some things I bought there—little knick knacks, mostly. But there were fly swatters, kitchen tools, and a wide variety of decorative items. Some of the department heads thought it was a waste of space but Mr. Clymer said that table brought people into the store.

The other big store in town was Scheetz's. They sold mostly furniture, bedding and linens. That was across the street from the courthouse on Court Street.

Henry had been working at J.J. Conroy Ford and learning to fly at Doylestown Airport. Conroy's also sold airplanes as a side business and Henry sold planes along with Bob Conroy. Soon Henry had his pilot's license and his own airplane.

We were married in 1938 at the Reformed Church (now Salem United Church of Christ) in Doylestown by Dr. Freeman. Our first home was on Ashland Avenue where it joins State Street. There we had our first child in 1941. Many times on a Sunday we would go to church and then fly to Ocean City, New Jersey, swim in the ocean, lie on the beach and head home before it was dark.

Clymer's Department Store

And then came Pearl Harbor. Henry enlisted in the Army and became a flight instructor. He was assigned first to Pottstown, Pennsylvania, where I was able to join him. Then he went to Reading. I returned to Doylestown and continued as a housewife and mother. But I also was active in the Red Cross, helping out with what we today call the Bloodmobile. I had a uniform and one of our responsibilities was preparing meals for the doctors and nurses who drew the blood. We charged thirty-five cents for the meals.

After the war, Henry returned home and continued his work with Conroy Ford. He had started as a window cleaner and gradually worked himself up through the various departments to sales and, finally, he had his own dealership.

"Vicky Victory"
your
HAIR AID warden
says!
save steel
USE YOUR
VICTORY HAIR PIN KIT
AGAIN and AGAIN!
Take it to the BEAUTY SALON
every time you go!

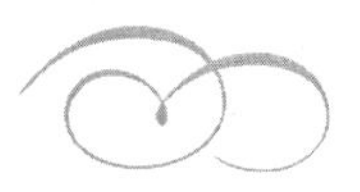

Vivian Paist Crouthamel

Vivian and her husband live in Chalfont, Pennsylvania, and have a daughter, Susan, and two married grandchildren. Vivian loves to read. She is active in her church and she volunteers at the local hospital.

I graduated from Norristown High School in 1940 and moved to Doylestown, Pennsylvania, along with my mother. Since my father had died when I was a child, Mother had to work to provide for her three children. The three of us spent many vacations in Doylestown with our grandparents. Early in the war, my brother was called up in the Army and served with the infantry in Europe. He and three other men were scouts who crossed the Rhine River into Germany in order to provide intelligence for their superiors. My sister's husband was also in the Army, so she and her child moved from Washington, D C., and came to live with us. Prior to the birth of her child, my sister had been a driver for the Red Cross.

My first job was as a sales clerk in Musselman's Department Store in Doylestown. After a short while I became their bookkeeper. I remained at Musselman's for seven months. Then I accepted a job at The Doylestown National Bank and Trust Company as a title stenographer.

Vivian (left) and sister Sarah Mueller

Just about all the young men were in the service, as was my future husband. We were married Labor Day Weekend in 1943 on his short leave. The wedding was at St. Paul's Episcopal Church. Because of the gasoline shortage, everyone walked from the church to the Doylestown Inn for the reception.

Because of the gasoline shortage, everyone walked from the church to the Doylestown Inn for the reception.

My husband was stationed at Xavier University in Cincinnati, Ohio, as a supply sergeant. Before I moved to Cincinnati to be with him I flew out several weekends. My husband was sharing an apartment with another soldier. I loved graham cracker pie so I thought I would bake one. I was just a bride. I made the pie, but the crust was also the filling with meringue on top. I was real pleased with myself since the pie looked so nice. Actually I couldn't cook worth a darn. The poor fellows couldn't get their forks through the pie, but they were polite and tried to eat it. I was so embarrassed!

In Cincinnati we lived in a large room with a shared bath in a lovely old home. Since the Army paid for our accommodations and food, we ate at restaurants every night.

Once settled in our large room, I started working at Procter and Gamble (P&G) in the typing pool. The company had a policy of sending a box of all their products to new employees. Living in one room, I could hardly use any of these items, so I shipped them

The company had employed only men for supervisory positions, and these new women supervisors had to sign a form stating they would relinquish their positions when the men returned from service

home and had them ready when I started housekeeping at a later date.

I had a woman supervisor at P&G. Until that time, the company had employed only men for supervisory positions. These new women supervisors had to sign a form stating they would relinquish their positions when the men returned from service. I don't know if this actually happened, but I suspect it did.

I was transferred from the typing pool to the Finance Department and kept the books that contained the deductions for War Bonds of every P&G employee throughout the United States. Each month I had to total the books. On July 1 the books came out exactly right—the first time that had ever happened.

The very next day, my husband received his transfer papers from the Air Force to the Infantry. He was to be shipped to Europe shortly. I decided to leave P&G to return home. When news of my leaving the company reached the office of the Vice President, he called and asked me to stay at least several more months. But I was homesick and didn't want to stay in Cincinnati alone.

I returned to my former position at the bank. A director of the bank who was the head of the Rationing Board asked if I would like to work at the Rationing Board. It was a temporary Civil Service job. I took it because the pay was better and the longer hours would keep me busy while my husband was in Europe. Although local businessmen volunteered their time to be in charge of each category—such as sugar, tires, and gasoline—Civil Servant clerks did much of the work. I worked in fuel oil. When stamps were returned, each night two different clerks went downstairs to the furnace to burn the returned stamps.

While working at the Rationing Board I occasionally returned to Musselman's. The owner had asked several of us former employees to help out during the holidays, particularly on weekends and evenings.

The town rallied around the war effort and people felt close to one another—almost like family. People went to church more often and War Bond rallies were held on the court house lawn. Oscar Hammerstein was the guest at one of the rallies.

Through the Junior Women's Club I was on the planning committee for a dance at the Doylestown Country Club for a convoy of soldiers passing through town. One of the favorite songs back then was "The Boogie Woogie Bugler Boy." I also knit a brown sweater for the Red Cross. I blocked it too wide and too short, which I guess is the reason they never asked me to do another one.

I had the opportunity to see several famous performers. In Cincinnati, I saw Vaughan Monroe on stage, and Jan Pierce singing "The Bluebird of Happiness." At the Philadelphia Academy of Music I saw Oscar Levant in performance, and I also attended the first performance of *Oklahoma* in Philadelphia.

When V-J Day came and the war finally ended, I was in Atlantic City, New Jersey, with my husband who had just returned from Europe. I recall his saying, "If you survive the first day in battle, you know you'll survive the war." We thought his leave would be brief because he had orders to ship out to Japan but, fortunately, his tour of duty was cancelled.

The country breathed a great sigh of relief, welcomed back our servicemen, and prepared for a huge housing boom to accommodate the young couples reunited and ready to begin raising families.

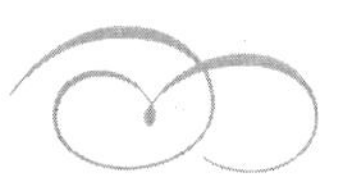

Esther Shutt Fellman

Esther was born on the property that is now Central Bucks South High School in Warrington, Pennsylvania. She died in 1995. Her daughter, Suzanne, spent many happy hours listening to the stories of her mother's life.

As told to her daughter Suzanne Fellman Jacob of Chalfont, PA.

I graduated from Doylestown High School in 1940 with a concentration in the Commercial course. That meant I could do secretarial work, but the summer of 1940 was a difficult time to find a job. The Depression was still influencing the job market. Even though Hitler had invaded Poland in September 1939 and Europe was at war, it didn't mean this area of Bucks County was gearing up for war. Far from it.

I wanted a job in Doylestown, but since my home was on Folly Road in Warrington Township, I would need to find a ride or use public transportation, which was some distance away from my home. My older siblings were of little help since no one was working in Doylestown. My oldest brother, Frank, helped Dad (G. Leroy Shutt) run the farm. My sister, Marietta, though very bright was limited to jobs near home because of severe bouts of psoriasis, which she had on a recurring basis. My sister, Virginia, was in nursing school in Philadelphia. And my youngest brother, Bud (Leroy W. Shutt), was still at Doylestown High School.

The summer of 1940 did not portend what was going to happen in 1941 when our country was at war.

Esther and Merrill on their wedding day, March 11, 1946

Even though Hitler had invaded Poland in September 1939 and Europe was at war, it didn't mean this area of Bucks County was gearing up for war. Far from it.

I had to pound the pavements in search of a job and finally, after several months, I found one with a Doylestown lawyer. After school started in September, Bud and I occasionally took the family car or Frank would drive us to Doylestown. We often rode our bikes out Folly Road to Bristol Road and then to Route 611. We parked our bikes in back of the Warrington Store and hopped the bus to Doylestown.

And then Frank became sick—very sick. He was dying of a rare form of blood disease. Dr. Moore of Doylestown got the press to cover Frank's situation and someone who had survived the disease offered his blood for a transfusion. A very pretty nurse, Doris Bates, was one of his caregivers. They were married in April, 1941. Between Frank's illness and

Dr. Moore of Doylestown got the press to cover Frank's situation, and someone who had survived the disease offered his blood for a transfusion.

then his wedding plans, I had a lot on my mind.

Marietta's future husband, Stanley Detweiler of Chalfont, was inducted in February of 1941 and went to Fort Knox, Kentucky for basic training and then to Pine Camp, New York. Stan obtained a short leave at the end of December 1941, following the attack at Pearl Harbor. Knowing that he was bound for overseas duty, Marietta and Stan were married at 1:00 a.m. January 1, 1942. I was so proud to be her maid of honor. I wore a gold crepe dress with brown accessories and a corsage of mixed flowers. Marietta was in a powder blue wool crepe street-length dress with black accessories. Her corsage was white mums and snapdragons. What a way to celebrate the New Year! Since the war news was so depressing, seeing them so happy made us feel happy for awhile. And even though it was just the immediate families that attended, it was a wonderful holiday.

My sister, Virginia, enlisted in the Army Nurse Corps in 1943. She served in the European Theatre of Operations, landing at Normandy Beach shortly after the first wave of servicemen went ashore. Because she was on a surgical team, her hours were long and her duty stations always near the front. She was awarded a Bronze Star for her performance during the Battle of Bulge, but it was decades before she told us she had received the award.

Even though working in the law office wasn't really challenging or fun, I loved working in Doylestown. Several of my high school classmates also worked in Doylestown and we would meet every so often at the Rexall Drug Store counter for a talk-filled lunch. If I had no one to eat lunch with, I'd pack my lunch and eat it while walking through Doylestown. Shopping at Scheetz's Department Store was always fun, but I did more window shopping than actual buying.

I joined the Book-of-the-Month Club and read Bernard deVoto's *Year of Decision 1846*, Margaret Leech's *Reveille in Washington*, most of the *Zane Grey* series, *Kabloona*, and even *Bambi*. *Bartlett's Quotations* was used by my daughter well into the 1980s and remains one of her most valued books, even though later editions of the book were printed. After I was married and there was no money for books, those editions purchased during my "affluent war years" stayed in our house and many of them went to my daughter.

Esther's sister Virginia Shutt, U.S. Army Nurse Corps

One of my other pleasures during this period was purchasing and planting flowers. I was able to obtain roses and planted them around my parents' home. I also purchased irises and other perennials. Working in the garden relaxed me, got me out in the sun, and made me realize how much my farmer parents had taught me about working the soil and letting nature do its thing.

In mid-1941, I heard through the grapevine about a clerical position in the office of the Doylestown Draft Board. I had to go to Philadelphia to take a Civil Service exam and I was a nervous wreck. I hated the city and I resented the additional tension of traveling to Philadelphia. But I typed very well, had clear handwriting, and passed with enough points to obtain the job.

It was an introductory position. Initially, there were two of us in the Draft Board office located in the Bucks County Courthouse in the center of Doylestown. Eventually, Emily Clymer of Doylestown joined us and she and I became fast and good working companions and friends. It was hard and demanding work. The paperwork on each man had to be correct, and files had to be maintained carefully as the government demanded exactness. But we delivered and, on occasion, had fun doing it. Emily was as hard a worker as anyone I've ever met.

Some days I had to work overtime to prepare paperwork for departing men or to ready reports that the government required, and Emily usually stayed with me. However, there were times that I locked up the office by myself but I was never afraid because there was so much activity going on in the Courthouse. We had round-the-clock coverage in the clock tower with Civil Defense plane spotters posted there throughout most of the war. Even Dad participated in that job.

Making decisions concerning young men who claimed the status of Conscientious Objector was not easy. I was glad the local Draft Board (all men) made the decision. Some of the men who claimed that status were not only entitled to it but often participated in the war effort by serving in civilian hospitals or in other positions unrelated to the war. But some men just did not want to leave home, or their parents did not want them to leave home, so they claimed a religious deferment. Because the Board members were local people, draftees unjustly claiming deferment usually did not succeed in their bid.

We had round-the-clock coverage in the clock tower with Civil Defense plane spotters posted there throughout most of the war.

Draft Board members felt it was their duty to see each group of men depart Doylestown but on occasion none of the members could attend. So I substituted. I would go down to the Doylestown train station, make sure all the paperwork was in order and see that the new draftees were prepared to board the train on the first leg of their journey into military service.

In 1943 I became eligible to vote and I registered as a Republican, the same as my parents. It was exciting to be able to vote.

When I received my first War Ration Book I felt proud to be helping the war effort. This, in addition to my job, was my small contribution—along with all other Americans—to help our fighting men and women. We all had family and friends overseas who we worried about. But we also knew they didn't have what we had here at home. So this small Ration Book served as a constant reminder of their sacrifice on our behalf.

I met Merrill Fellman of Chalfont through the young people's organization of the Chalfont Grange where our parents were members. There were many activities offered for us young people at the Grange and also at our churches. I was a member of Pleasantville Reformed Church (later United Church of Christ) at Limekiln Pike and County Line Road in

This small Ration Book served as a constant reminder of their sacrifice on our behalf.

Warrington Township, and Merrill was a member of St. Peter's Lutheran Church in Hilltown, Pennsylvania. Even though there was rationing and a war going on, we still had fun dating and getting to know one another. Merrill was 4-F because of a heart murmur, which never seemed to bother him in later life.

And so it went through the war. I worked hard and enjoyed my gardening, reading, and dating. Merrill came to my home by bike. It was a long ride from his home in Chalfont to Folly Road. Often we would stay around home but sometimes a group of us from church would pedal to Whitemarsh Cemetery in Horsham where we could walk around the grounds, admire the bell tower (also used for plane spotting), and enjoy a great afternoon in the sun.

After the war's end, my work began to wind down and it became less intense. Gone were the late hours as men started coming home from their overseas assignments. But my job remained intact for awhile. In order to ensure peace, new draftees were needed to replace the returning servicemen, now reunited with their families after years of separation.

In March 1946, Merrill and I were married in a quiet ceremony at my church with only our immediate families in attendance. We traveled to Baltimore, Maryland for our honeymoon.

Due to constraints still in effect by the Office of Price Administration, rental property fees were frozen at a certain level. The monthly rent for our first apartment, located on the corner of Victory Avenue (now Maple Avenue) and Main Street (Route 152N) in Chalfont, was $41.00. The Tenant's Copy of that rental agreement remains in my personal papers. It would take us several months to obtain a refrigerator, but we were in love and didn't care. Besides, many people had more problems than we did.

In mid-1946, I was told the Draft Board would be closed down. Emily and I began the arduous process of packing files and paperwork for shipment to government storage. Furniture was sold and the office reverted to Bucks County. Years later, the office trash can that I purchased served as a waste can in our home. I also purchased my office typewriter, which I used until I could no longer type. Both items reminded me of busy but happy years in that job. When the office finally closed, I received a lovely watch from the Draft Board. It was worn with pride of a job well done—a job necessary for America's survival.

Not all of the men that I processed through the office came home. Some were buried overseas, some were buried at sea, and others came back injured. But I never regretted my role in the Draft Board. In fact, I don't remember any family or individual ever telling me they did not like what I had done. Everyone recognized I was the face behind the paperwork but not the ultimate instrument of their family member's death or their going overseas. That could only be laid, squarely and fairly, at the feet of Adolf Hitler, Benito Mussolini, and the military cabal that dominated Japan.

In the 1960s when the old Bucks County Courthouse was torn down to make way for the new one, I took my daughter with me to watch as they swung the huge wrecking ball through my office. As the ball hit the outer wall and crumbled through into the office area, tears streamed down my face. A way of life—years of privation but happiness and the memories of voices going up the steps to the watchtower, of Emily asking me a question, of two typewriters pounding away—flew around in my mind as the ball destroyed the office. Suzanne gently took my hand and her closeness helped me through those awful moments. Then I wiped my eyes, drew myself up, gripped her hand firmly and said it was time to go home and prepare supper. We walked down Main Street to our little house on Hillside Avenue with barely a word spoken.

The next day Suzanne brought me a piece of the old Courthouse that had fallen outside the protecting fence. I like to think it came from my area. The stone, the typewriter, the trashcan, and the watch are a reminder of my small contribution to the larger war effort. They were good years and the job was great. What a wonderful experience for a young woman!

Civil Defense Badge

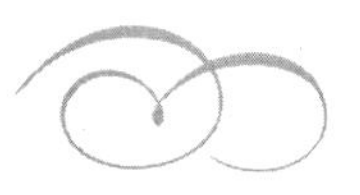

Martha Eleonora Skoog

Martha was born in Plainfield, New Jersey, and has been a resident of Bucks County since 1931. In retirement she has enjoyed volunteering, traveling, writing family history, painting, carving, and embroidering.

When Pearl Harbor occurred in 1941, I was a senior day student at Beaver College in Jenkintown, Pennsylvania (now Arcadia University, Glenside). I commuted on the Reading Railroad from Doylestown. My father drove me three miles to the station each morning and met me there in the evening.

At the train station in the morning, it was sad to see groups of draftees and recruits saying goodbye to their families as they headed off for basic training. As the war progressed the bold headlines on the daily papers were frightening and overwhelming. On the radio we heard Adolf Hitler's ranting speeches as well as Winston Churchill's defiant determination not to give up. Stories of Hitler's youth camps and indoctrination were terrifying.

Martha in 1941

Following graduation I began working at the Federal Reserve Bank of Philadelphia (Third Federal Reserve District) in the Consumer Credit Department, which had been created to regulate the extension of credit to individuals. Within a few months I was transferred to the Research Department as secretary to the Director of Research. The department collected all kinds of economic data and prepared reports for the Board of Directors and the president of the Bank. This served as background information when the presidents of the twelve District Banks met with members of the Board of Governors and the Chairman of the Federal Reserve System in Washington, D.C., to develop monetary policy at the Federal Open Market Committee meetings held every three weeks.

On the radio we heard Adolf Hitler's ranting speeches as well as Winston Churchill's defiant determination not to give up.

In July of 1944, my boss, Karl R. Bopp, was a delegate to the United Nations Monetary and Financial Conference at Bretton Woods, New Hampshire, which led to the establishment of the International Monetary Fund in 1947, and the creation of the International Bank for Reconstruction and Development in 1946. The purpose of these actions was to help eliminate poverty in the world and to minimize future world economic instability. Mr. Bopp returned with boxes of materials and then I was assigned to organize and catalog them.

The Federal Reserve System was responsible for financing the war effort

In 1943 the Federal Reserve Banks were declared "essential," implying that we were frozen in our jobs.

through issuance of Treasury bills, notes and bonds, and it conducted at least six war savings bond drives over the years. As employees, we were expected to invest in Series E bonds through payroll deductions. In 1943 the Federal Reserve Banks were declared "essential," implying that we were frozen in our jobs. Years later I was appointed head of the Public Services and Consumer Affairs Department.

In Doylestown many civilians served as airplane spotters, watching the night sky from the vantage point of the tower on the old courthouse. Women rolled bandages, knit sweaters and took courses in first aid in case of an emergency. One of our church members, Virginia Lewis, ran her husband's gasoline station while he was in the service.

Our men and women in the armed forces were very much on the minds and prayers of our churches. Six of them from our church, Salem United Church of Christ (then Salem Evangelical and Reformed Church) gave their lives. Our pastor, Dr. Charles F. Freeman, in a January 1943 letter to the congregation wrote:

"1943 is going to be a hard, trying year for everyone. Not one will escape. The role to be played by your church and religion is no minor one...Our chief interest in 1943 will be with the men and women in the armed forces, their families, and with all who are called upon to suffer more than we on account of the war. Our program will be (1) to keep in close and frequent contact with our soldier members, (2) their families and (3) to provide money to feed, clothe, and relieve prisoners and starving men, women, and children in foreign countries and at home."

Also in January of 1943, requests for cots and other materials appeared in the church bulletin. Doylestown Hospital asked our church to be ready to serve as an emergency hospital in case of a catastrophe in the town. In March of 1943, Salem donated a Chaplain's Field Communion Set and at Christmas sent boxes of goodies to our servicemen and one woman.

A special music program was held when hymns requested by our military people were featured. Among those songs requested by specific persons were "Onward Christian Soldiers," "Eternal Father, Strong to Save"

Martha (far left) at Federal Reserve Christmas party

(Navy hymn), "My Faith Looks Up to Thee," "Now the Day is Over," "The Old Rugged Cross," "Holy, Holy, Holy," "Love Divine, All Loves Excelling," "Dear Lord and Father of Mankind," "Stand Up, Stand Up for Jesus," and "All Hail the Power of Jesus' Name."

At the close of the war, Protestant churches of America planned to raise $50,000,000 for overseas relief and rehabilitation over a four-year period. Our denomination was challenged to raise $2,000,000.

It was at the close of the war that the Heifer Project made its first shipment of heifers overseas. One of our church members, George Shelly, was among the first persons to accompany heifers to Germany.

There was much to be done to rehabilitate those countries devastated by war. Our country—as individuals, as churches and other organizations, and as a government—rose to the challenge.

THE CONGREGATION OF
The Salem Evangelical and Reformed Church
DOYLESTOWN, PA.
PRESENTS
A Vesper Service of Request Hymns
(FROM OUR MEN IN SERVICE)
Sunday afternoon, October 10, 1943
AT FOUR O'CLOCK
IN HONOR OF
Our Men and Women in Service

Special music program honoring men and women in the service

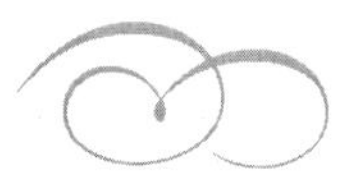

Helen Wachter Schmidt

Having lived through two world wars, as well as recent localized wars, Helen appreciates our nation's freedom. She feels that life in our country has been good to her, and she sees a greater future ahead for our youth.

I grew up in Richmond Hills, Queens in New York. In 1931, I graduated from Brown's Business College at a time when jobs were very difficult to find. It was the height of the Great Depression. My father worked as a draftsman at Mergenthaler Lynotype in Brooklyn, where the company was on a limited schedule—one week on and one week off. At least he received a salary as opposed to many people. Also, my older sister, Beatrice, was working for New York Edison and she contributed to the family income.

Several years after I graduated, Mergenthaler Lynotype hired me to work in the Complaints Department. I received letters and phone calls from customers who were having difficulties with equipment. Times were still difficult during the 1930s, but once war was imminent, the company's products were in great demand for the war effort. During the war years, my father worked ten hours a day, six days a week. Since my work was considered defense work, I received a special certificate at the end of the war lauding me for my contribution to the war effort.

Helen in 1942

As soon as war was declared, New York City changed dramatically almost overnight.

On land owned by Mergenthaler Lynotype, the United States government opened a new factory dedicated primarily to grinding lens for bombsights. Since tool and die workers were in great demand, a number of regular employees from Mergenthaler Lynotype went to work in the new factory. After the war, the Veterans Administration took over the building and Mergenthaler Lynotype was forced to take the workers back.

As soon as war was declared, New York City changed dramatically almost overnight. All stores, including grocery stores, closed at 6:00 p.m. Fifteen-watt bulbs replaced higher wattage bulbs on the elevated lines and at nighttime, Broadway appeared dead even though shows continued throughout the war years. And, of course, blackout window shades were standard on all homes and businesses. The goal was to prevent any glow from New York City to be visible from the skies and from the ocean.

Women took over many tasks—in the factories, as bus drivers, and as air raid wardens. The wardens came around

Mothers Pledge to Keep the Home Fires Burning

New York Journal and American
CHARACTER QUALITY ENTERPRISE ACCURACY
AN AMERICAN PAPER FOR THE AMERICAN PEOPLE
TUESDAY, MAY 6, 1941 13

2nd FRONT PAGE
The JOURNAL-AMERICAN HAS TWO FRONT PAGES DAILY

Pledged to keep the home fires burning, members of the newly-formed Home Legion, composed of mothers, wives, sisters and sweethearts of the boys who answered Uncle Sam's call, are seen at stirring organization rally at Hotel Astor. Some 1,500 women from all walks of life heard Mrs. Margaret Irving James, wife of an officer at Camp Upton, outline plans for best serving menfolk in various camps; and also forming a second line of defense for Uncle Sam. Above you see just part of the great throng that filled ballroom to launch this patriotic movement with unsurpassed enthusiasm. WMCA broadcast

Helen (left front) joins with other New York City women to show support for our troops

to houses to make sure our homes were prepared for an emergency. In case of fires, we all were required to keep a bucket of sand in our basements. Many of us took first aid courses to be able to administer help to victims of an enemy attack.

On May 8, 1945, my mother died during gall bladder surgery. Many of the finest doctors were in the service, making it sometimes difficult for civilians to receive adequate care.

As a result of my mother's death, I became responsible for the food shopping for my father and myself since my sister had married and had her own home. I had a lot to learn and think about as I set out for groceries considering the fact that many products were rationed including sugar, meat, and butter. A shop in Queens allowed you to buy all the fish and chicken you wanted, so naturally we ate lots of fish and chicken.

A friend who worked at the Brooklyn Navy Yard, across the street from Mergenthaler Lynotype, invited me to the commissioning of the battleship U.S.S. *North Carolina* on April 9, 1941. I took off from work for part of the day and had a wonderful time. I later learned that the ship was considered to be the world's greatest sea weapon at that time, engaging in twelve major battles in the Pacific Theater. It was a huge ship, manned by 144 commissioned officers and 2,195 enlisted men.

We all had friends and neighbors in the armed forces. One family had three sons in the service, but the younger one was given a deferment to care for their mother who had tuberculosis. However, when the need for more draftees became necessary, it was determined that his mother could live on the money being sent home from the remaining sons, so the fourth son was also drafted. The older sons all survived the war, but the younger one was killed three months into his service. He was a gunner on an oil tanker that collided with another ship in the Atlantic Ocean.

As difficult as life was in some respects, we still had time for entertainment. There was no admission fee at the zoo or at any of the museums. Many summer days were spent at Jones Beach listening to the Guy Lombardo band and enjoying the other pleasures of the beach. Strict regulations prohibited amusements and shops other than those providing food. Behind the boardwalk were beautiful flower gardens. Much credit goes to Robert Moses, New York City Parks Commissioner, who greatly expanded the city and state park system, creating hundreds of playgrounds and recreational facilities.

RCA Radio Studios provided us with opportunities to see the Big Bands on stage. With the help of a friend's sister who worked at the ticket office, we managed to see Benny Goodman, Harry James, and other popular orchestras of the day.

During the war years, there was a popular song, "When the Lights Go On Again All Over the World." For us New Yorkers, those lights went on again on Broadway at the close of the war. And what a grand celebration!

Women as military wives

June Grim Renville

June and Bob reared three children while Bob continued to work for the U.S. Government serving in Turkey, the Philippines and Brazil. June has lived in Florida for over thirty years and enjoys volunteering at a local elementary school.

I grew up in the community of Lincoln University, Chester County, Pennsylvania, where my father taught biology, anatomy, and botany in the H. F. Grim Science Building, named for him in his later years at the college. When he first went to Lincoln in 1912, he taught Greek, Latin, and German, but was soon made a science professor. During the war years, he was in the classroom during the day and then drove the half-hour to Wilmington, Delaware, every evening to work a full eight-hour shift at the Du Pont Company's munitions factory. It was quite common for people to have more than one job, particularly when the work was related to the war effort.

After graduating from Yale School of Nursing, my sister Elizabeth enlisted in the Army Nurse Corps. She worked in psychiatric services for returning servicemen at a hospital in Hartford, Connecticut.

It was at Bucknell University in Lewisburg, Pennsylvania during the late 1930s that I met my husband Bob. He had arrived at college during our junior year since he had first gone to a junior college. When I saw him come into the classroom, I noted to a classmate that he looked "pretty good." A date was arranged for us to attend a dance and we were married in 1940, after graduating in 1938. Bob had served as a government intern in Washington, D. C., and I taught Latin and French in New Castle, Delaware.

One of my tasks was to transcribe stories on tape that had been dictated by pilots returning from the Pacific area following the attack on Pearl Harbor.

June and Bob's wedding day, 1940

After our marriage, we moved to Washington where Bob worked for the War Production Board in the Budget and Planning Department and I worked for the Red Cross as a filing clerk. When I learned that the War Department was looking for stenographers, I applied and was hired to work in the Army Air Corps section. One of my tasks was to transcribe stories on tape that had been dictated by pilots returning from the Pacific area following the attack on Pearl Harbor.

Bob enlisted in the Navy

During 1942 and early into 1943, one hundred and eleven ships were attacked by German U-boats and almost nine hundred men were killed or wounded within the Gulf of Mexico.

in July of 1942 and was assigned to the Gulf Sea Frontier. He was told he was to be in Miami but soon learned that the unit had not yet moved from Key West, so we went there for a few weeks and lived in a hotel. His work was the routing of convoys of ships carrying supplies and troops. He was comfortable with his work, but he had had no Navy training and was unfamiliar with Navy rules and regulations. So we stayed in the hotel every night because he said he didn't know who he was supposed to salute.

It was not until the end of the war in June of 1945 that the story of the Gulf Sea Frontier was told. During 1942 and early into 1943, one hundred and eleven ships were attacked by German U-boats and almost nine hundred men were killed or wounded within the Gulf of Mexico. Additionally, twenty-five ships were torpedoed off the coast of Florida, some within sight of luxury hotels. Our country had insufficient ships and planes to thwart these attacks!

So close were some of these U-boats that a torpedo missed hitting a ship at the mouth of the Mississippi River and lodged in the levee. Within sight of land, burning ships could be seen off the coast of Florida. It wasn't until late in 1943, after sufficient planes, ships, and blimps had been produced, that we were able to put a stop to this menace.

Within a few weeks after arriving in Key West, we moved to Miami where Bob continued his work with the Gulf Sea Frontier. The city was swarming with military. During the heat of the summer I recall seeing soldiers keel over from heat stroke during maneuvers. Their fellow soldiers just walked over or around them and left them lying on the ground. After the maneuvers were completed, someone would come back for the fallen men. During that time, I worked as a secretary to a Navy commander in the Du Pont Building.

I stopped working when our first child was born in 1942. We had the normal rationing problems and we soon tired of eating chicken. It seems that was about the only meat we could find. In order to conserve energy, Daylight Saving Time was inaugurated in February of 1942 and continued year round until after the war. I had heard that in England

German U-boats in the Gulf of Mexico

they actually had Double Daylight Savings Time—an extra two hours of daylight.

In 1944 Bob was sent to Leyte in the Philippines to do the same kind of work he had been doing—routing convoys. I returned to my parents' home in Pennsylvania to await the end of the war and Bob's return in 1946.

One day in early January of that year, I was playing bridge at a neighbor's house in Lincoln University when my mother called to say I had a telegram from Bob. He would be arriving in Wilmington the next afternoon. I couldn't keep my mind on bridge and was excused for the remainder of the day.

When Bob returned, he was assigned to the Civilian Production Administration as an Administrative Analyst in Washington. Housing was scarce and we felt ourselves fortunate to find a rental property on Columbia Pike in Arlington, Virginia. It was an old house with a coal furnace and our washing machine was of the old ringer type. Nevertheless, the war was over and we were happy to be together once again.

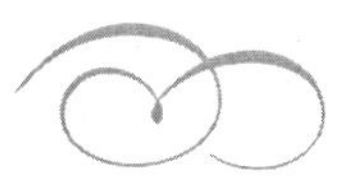

Minerva Bechtold Antal

Minerva now lives in Doylestown, Pennsylvania, after having shared in her husband's ministry for over forty years. Upon retirement, they both worked with Habitat for Humanity in locations from Florida to Arizona.

After graduating in 1938 from Indiana State Teachers College (now Indiana University of Pennsylvania), I returned to my hometown of Lancaster, Pennsylvania, to live with my parents. My mother was a housewife and my father was President of M.T. Garvins Department Store. His first job with the store had been as an errand boy.

I had it in my head that I would like to move to the big city of Philadelphia, but my father would not permit it. So I secured a job in the Bureau of Interior Decorating at Armstrong Linoleum and Cork Company. Our bureau set up rooms that were then photographed to appear in advertising catalogs.

One of my good friends attending Millersville State Teachers College (now Millersville University) was dating a ministerial student at the Evangelical and Reformed (E&R) Lancaster Seminary. She arranged a double date for me with another ministerial student, Art Antal, who later became my husband. On that first date we did not hit it off very well, but we persevered and within a few weeks we warmed up to one another.

One evening when the meat was particularly tough, I asked the waitress what we were being served. She said, "Horse." I still don't know if she was serious.

Since Art was of Hungarian descent, upon his graduation from seminary in 1941 he accepted a job at a Hungarian E&R church in Gary, Indiana. I stayed in Lancaster because of my job, but in 1943 we married. Shortly thereafter, he was accepted into the Army as a Chaplain. I went with him to Cambridge, Massachusetts, for his training at the Chaplain School at Harvard University. He lived in a dormitory and I lived in a boarding house. We ate dinners together at various restaurants. One evening when the meat was particularly tough, I asked the waitress what we were being served. She said, "Horse." I still don't know if she was serious.

Minerva, Beth and Art

Art was assigned to a unit that was sent to El Paso, Texas, before going on to Pitts-

We knew Art was in the thick of war activities, but we knew little else. His letters contained lots of blacked out sections.

burgh, California. Fortunately, I was able to be with him until his unit was shipped overseas to the Philippine Islands.

I returned to my parents' home in Lancaster to await the arrival of our first child, Beth, born in 1944. She was born in Lancaster General Hospital which had been founded by my grandfather, also an E&R minister. What a Godsend Beth was for our household. We knew Art was in the thick of war activities, but little else. His letters contained lots of blacked out sections. Even when he returned in November of 1945, he spoke very little about his wartime activities.

Upon his return Art made use of the GI Bill by attending Union Seminary at Columbia University for two years. Beth and I joined him as we resumed married life, thankful that the war years were behind us and we could look forward to a world at peace. And then, two more daughters, Kay and Margie, were welcomed into our busy family.

Minerva and Art on an ice skating date

A Gas Mask requires
1.11 pounds of rubber
A Life Raft requires
17 to 100 pounds of rubber
A Scout Car requires
306 pounds of rubber
A Heavy Bomber requires
1,825 pounds of rubber
America needs your
SCRAP RUBBER

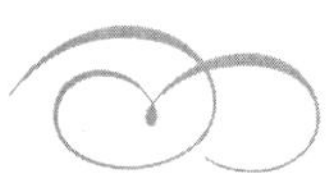

Margaret Auten Moorhead

Peg was born in Moresburg in central Pennsylvania. She was involved in music all her lif as a pianist and church organist. Peg died in 1992.

As told by her daughter, Besse Moorhead Brindle

In 1942 my father, Mellicent Scott Moorhead (Buck), and my mother, Margaret (Peg), were both teachers in the Midway school system near Pittsburgh. Peg taught music K-12 and directed the band. She had graduated from West Chester State Teachers College (now West Chester University) in 1941, and Buck had graduated from Washington and Jefferson College in 1937. They fell in love and were married July 11, 1942 in her hometown of Moresburg, a small town not too far from Danville, Pennsylvania.

As the United States' involvement in World War II grew and gas rationing became a fact of life, traveling long distances became difficult. No one from McDonald, the town where Buck lived in western Pennsylvania, was able to make the trip to central Pennsylvania for Buck and Peg's wedding. However, Buck's two aunts, Aunt Laura and Aunt Hilda, both in their later years, decided to give him a proper send-off to his wedding. As he boarded the train headed for Moresburg, they were on hand to throw rice at him.

Buck's little dog, Popeye, was the only "member" of his family to attend the wedding.

The only "member" of Buck's family to attend the wedding was his little dog, Popeye, and she was appropriately fitted with a big white bow for the occasion. Since there hadn't been a wedding in the church in forty years, and given the fact that the church was a public place, most of the community turned out for the event.

Peg and Buck

After returning to McDonald, the newlyweds resided at Aunt Hilda's. But their marital bliss was short-lived. Since Buck had already enlisted in the Army Air Corps, he was called up in January of 1943 and told to report to San Antonio, Texas, for pre-flight training. Peg remained in McDonald, living with her sister-in-law Julia and pursuing piano studies at Carnegie-Mellon in Pittsburgh while continuing to teach.

In the summer of 1943, Peg took the train to visit Buck in Texas. On her return trip, the express train on which she was traveling would actually take her through McDonald on the way to Pittsburgh. Once in Pittsburgh, she would then have to wait several hours for a local train to take her back to McDonald.

The conductor was a friendly old

He told her he would hop off the train and place her baggage on the platform, and all she had to do was jump carefully from the slowly moving train.

man. Not too long after the train left St. Louis he talked with Peg and learned the details of her journey. Realizing she would have a long wait in Pittsburgh, he arranged for the engineer to slow down the train as it passed through McDonald. He told her he would hop off the train and place her baggage on the platform, and all she had to do was jump carefully from the slowly moving train. He explained the sensation that occurs when you jump off a moving train onto a stationary platform and advised her to be very careful. She did indeed jump carefully and reclaimed her luggage successfully.

As Peg walked through town, suitcase in hand, people were most astonished to hear her story. Heretofore, the train had always zipped through their community each morning and they were amazed to see it travel so slowly on this particular day. One person after another commented, "But the train never stops here." My parents always attributed this kindness to the fact that she was a serviceman's wife.

Peg practicing at her piano

In December of 1943, Buck received his commission and returned to Pittsburgh. As he raced down the train platform in his new uniform, Peg noticed that he had forgotten to cut off the price tags and they fluttered in the breeze as he ran.

Buck returned to Texas for flight school. In January of 1944, realizing that Buck would soon be sent overseas, Peg resigned her teaching position, bought a 1939 Ford and drove from McDonald to El Paso. She dealt with engine trouble, difficult riders, and was forced by circumstance into purchasing two tires on the black market. She finally arrived in El Paso and was able to spend time with her husband until he left for the European Theater on Easter Sunday.

Stationed in England, Buck flew with the 492nd Bomb Group of the 8th Air Force. After completing more than twenty missions (two on D-Day), he was assigned to the 801st, a group known as the "Carpetbaggers." Their missions were all performed at night in planes painted black. Their cargo consisted of supplies and French citizens who had fled from the German occupation and now wanted to return to France as part of the French Resistance. People of all ages, including one elderly woman, were parachuted back into France under cover of night.

While Buck was overseas, Peg continued to live with Buck's sister, Julia, playing the piano for various community groups and frequently accompanying other musicians. Since Julia's husband was a doctor, he was frequently away making house calls, delivering babies and handling emergency situations. Peg and Julia had grown to recognize his footsteps as he came up the front steps and onto the porch, but when a stranger's footsteps were heard, they dreaded the thought it might be a telegram reporting bad news. Happily, no such telegram arrived.

Buck returned to the States in September of 1944 and was assigned to Fort Myers, Florida, flying navigation trainees. Peg joined him, again driving down in a second-hand car, this time a red Mercury coupe. While there, she underwent an emergency appendectomy and was placed on a maternity ward where the atmosphere was lively and loud. On his first visit following her surgery, Buck was wearing his fatigues, which gave no evidence of his recent combat experience. Peg's desperate plea to move her out of that ward prompted him to go home, put on his Class A's and return for another visit. When the staff saw him in full regalia, they immediately moved her to a quieter and more restful environment.

In the spring of 1945, Buck was transferred to California, again flying navigator trainees. In August of that year, he was discharged from the Army and took a teaching position at Bucknell University. They lived temporarily with Peg's family in Moresburg.

Along with many other veterans, in September of 1946, Buck made use of the GI Bill and began work on his MA in mathematics at Washington and Jefferson College in Washington, Pennsylvania, where I was born in 1947. He and Peg lived in a converted Army barracks. Then Buck went on to receive a PhD in Education from the University of Pittsburgh. After several positions in the public schools of western Maryland, he became a professor at Gettysburg College, where I grew up. Peg taught piano at home and played the organ at Gettysburg Presbyterian Church for many years.

When recounting stories of the war years, my parents frequently commented on the many acts of kindness shown to them because of my father's service to our country.

When a stranger's footsteps were heard, they dreaded the thought it might be a telegram reporting bad news.

Jean DeKalb Kraus

Jean lives in Sellersville, Pennsylvania, near her children, and keeps busy with part-time work, volunteering at church, AAUW (American Association of University Women) and V.I.A. (Village Improvement Association) while supporting community activities.

The Japanese attack on U.S. forces at Pearl Harbor occurred on December 7, 1941, just two months before my high school graduation. Several young men from my small graduating class of ninety-two students enlisted in one of the services immediately.

After completing classical studies at Abington High School, Pennsylvania, I matriculated in the secretarial course at Peirce Business College, also in Philadelphia. Two other classmates from Abington joined me, and we all completed the year's course in ten months.

My first secretarial position was with the U.S. Army Hearing Board in Philadelphia, Pennsylvania. Three months later I transferred to the FBI, having applied to both organizations and after having been investigated by each upon graduation from Peirce.

At the FBI, I was assigned to a stenographic pool of about ninety women, working six days a week, 9:00 a.m. to 6:00 p.m. Additionally, we were required to work late hours (i.e., noon to 9:00 p.m.) on a rotating basis. Also, we had to relieve each other on the switchboard.

Jean and Louis

One night a train crash on the old Pennsylvania Line (now Amtrak) near Philadelphia completely lit up the switchboard. Sabotage was suspected!

One night a train crash on the old Pennsylvania Line near Philadelphia completely lit up the switchboard. Sabotage was suspected!

In the senior year of high school I had met my future husband. I was sixteen and he was nineteen. After high school and trade school, Louis worked in Bristol, Pennsylvania for Fleetwings, a company that built aircraft. There he rose to a supervisory position. He was always so proud of the C-130 cargo plane produced for the war effort.

We became engaged in April 1943, anticipating a wedding the following spring, but by fall of 1943, with the U.S. war effort in Germany and in the Pacific at its height, Louis's name

I was glad I could continue to feel part of the war effort with my work at the FBI.

came up in the draft. Prior to that time he had been deferred because he was working in a vital industry.

So we said goodbye in December of 1943 when he left for Navy Boot Camp in Sampson, New York. I was glad I could continue to feel part of the war effort with my work at the FBI.

Anticipating a ten-day leave at the end of his training at Sampson, Louis asked me to consider marriage before he shipped overseas. My mother was the romantic in the family and agreed to put together a wedding in three weeks! We were married on February 3, 1944 on a beautiful sunny winter day at Abington Presbyterian Church.

Friends in our age group were scattered because of the war, so it was a small wedding with a catered reception at my parents' lovely home in Overlook Hills. A number of my high school friends were able to attend and some new friends from the FBI. Missing were the men who were away at war.

Because of gas rationing we could not travel far, but our honeymoon in an historic hotel in Atlantic City was wonderful. It ended with our driving up the White Horse Pike in a snowstorm while my mother was awaiting our arrival for a dinner with my new in-laws!

Young and naive as I was, I had hoped to be able to accompany my husband in the service. That was not to be. Louis had additional training at a Navy installation in South Carolina and then took the long train ride across the country to San Diego where he was assigned to the Armed Guard of the U.S. Navy. This service protected merchant ships as they delivered vital supplies throughout the Pacific Theater of War.

Since mail coming from the Pacific was transmitted only when the ship came into port, we could go as long as two months without receiving mail. Most of the time we had no idea where Louis was. I sent letters every day, but had no way of knowing whether he received them. A strange way to start married life.

Regretfully, I had left the FBI to be married and took several months off until I knew where Louis was going to be. After he left for overseas, I took a secretarial position with a drug company since I could not return to the FBI after I was married. The official reason was that they were downsizing, but a friend told me it was because I was married.

The war began to hit home when two men from our area died about the time of the Battle of the Bulge. One was the husband of a close friend and the other a high school classmate.

For me, October 1944 was the most stressful time. We had not heard from Louis for quite awhile and we knew there was a lot of action around the Philippine Islands. His ship was in port and went down during the Battle of Leyte Bay. This proved fortuitous, allowing him to have a month's leave as a result of being without a ship. So we had a second honeymoon—this time in New York City where we were treated royally because he was in uniform. Tickets to shows and a temporary apartment were made available to us. It was a very special time.

All too soon my husband was back in the Pacific Theater, still with the Navy Armed Guard, but this time on an oil tanker with ports of call in Australia and in the Persian Gulf as well as in many Pacific islands.

In the meantime, I continued secretarial work at National Drug Company and later accepted a position in Philadelphia with ITCA (International Typographic Composition Association), a businessmen's organization. My father's company was a member. During the war I continued living at home with my parents and my maternal grandmother. My younger brother was also in the service and was in both Army and Navy training programs while attending Penn State. Fortunately, the war was over before he saw any action.

There was gas rationing and food rationing during these war years and we used public transportation as much as possible. To commute to the city, I took a bus to the Reading Railroad at Noble Station in Abington. We also learned to darken our windows at night and we experienced air raid drills. Some people in our neighborhood built bomb shelters and most of us stored extra canned goods in our basements.

Jean and her parents with Victory Garden

We were elated that the war ended quickly after the atomic bombs were used to defeat Japan, but in retrospect I wish my country had not unleashed this dreadful devastation on the world. In fact, later history books have concluded these bombings were not necessary to end the war.

So with great relief to all, the servicemen came home. Louis arrived just before Christmas 1945, having spent almost two years in the Pacific. It was quite an experience for a young man who had never been away from home before. It took several months for him to regain his health. He was thin and had developed a fungus infection all over his body, probably the result of extreme temperature change. Our regular physician did not know how to treat it, but we found a doctor who had seen fungus in the European Theater of War and he was a tremendous help.

Housing was not an option for us. There was none. I regret that we needed to stay with Mother and Dad but we no had choice. I worried about being an extra burden to them, so we made plans to build a house as soon as possible. We were fortunate to find ground nearby, and as a veteran Louis had priority for building materials. We were able to purchase the first refrigerator delivered in Willow Grove, Pennsylvania, after the war! (During the war, all the manufacturers of home appliances had converted to producing war materiel.) Our duplex home was ready for occupancy in the spring of 1947. Louis went back to work at Fleetwings in Bristol while I continued my secretarial work.

It was a strange way to start married life—living with parents, two years of separation, and then getting used to being together again. However, we survived the tough times, raised two daughters, and developed our four-acre property in Pipersville, Pennsylvania, where we eventually celebrated fifty-six years of marriage.

During some of those years and after our daughters had graduated from college, I turned my attention to my own long-sought-after goal of a college degree. Over a period of eight years, through a combination of night courses, correspondence courses and two summer residencies at Marywood College in Scranton, Pennsylvania, I received a B.S. degree in Business Administration. This degree enabled me to have a successful career of over fifty years in the business world.

YOUR VICTORY GARDEN
counts more than ever!

Women overseas

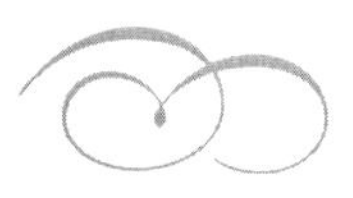

Marga Michel Scharmacher

Marga came to the United States in 1955. All she wanted was a peaceful life. She resides in Doylestown, Pennsylvania, where she enjoys her cat and gardening.

For many years of my life, I lived in Remscheid, Germany in North Rhine-Westphalia. Upon receiving my certificate from school in 1936, I went to work for Wurttembergische Metallwarenfabrik (WMF), a very large company that manufactured and sold fine crystal, silver and various articles for the home. The company is still in existence today. Back in the 1930s, it had stores in almost every German town of over one hundred thousand people. My first job was selling and cleaning the silver and delivering the products. The second year I was with the company, I was promoted to bookkeeping and window decorating. We had to learn our trade for three years in order to receive our examination papers.

The manager of my store was also manager of a WMF store in Solingen, which was opposite Remscheid on another mountain. Between the two towns was the Wupper River flowing through the town of Wuppertael. When the war started, I did the bookkeeping for the store in Solingen also, traveling every day by train across a very high bridge, one of the longest and highest in Europe at that time. In 1941, the store manager entered the army, leaving me responsible for the store.

For many years of my life, I lived in Remscheid, Germany in North Rhine-Westphalia.

Marga managing the store

Along with my job at WMF, I was also assigned to work in a health clinic for half a day. The government conscripted all able-bodied people for essential duty.

Before the war, my father had a little business making ice skates made of wood with leather straps to hold the skates in place and a piece of metal for the blade. The ice skates were used mostly in Holland because of the many waterways. He also made screwdrivers.

My brother was in the army, serving in France and Russia. He was wounded in the shoulder while in Russia, but recovered enough to spend the last days of the war as a soldier near Aachen, Germany. He then became a

Our town was bombed by the Allies a number of times. My sister had been enlisted to work in the police department, and helped warn the town of the approach of bombers.

prisoner of war for six months in France.

Our town was bombed by the Allies a number of times. My sister had been enlisted to work in the police department, and helped warn the town of the approach of bombers. When that occurred, we would try to go to the basement of our homes or to a bunker. Our town was built partly on a rocky mountain so the bunker was fairly secure. It was built partly by French prisoners, but the bunker was never finished. These same French prisoners also shoveled snow.

In February of 1942 I was alone in the store during the night, taking inventory while the manager was on home vacation. I was in a little office with no windows. Around midnight, we had an air raid, which made lots of noise. The whole town was affected and many buildings were damaged including ours, which had five large display windows broken. I was very frightened. In the morning I was able to contact the manager, and he was able to make all the necessary repair arrangements.

Then, in June of 1943, we had a major air raid, lasting over an hour. When the warnings started, we looked out the window at the "Christmas tree." That's what we called the approaching planes because all we could see was a huge number of lights coming our way. We went to the basement and were there for an hour. Every minute felt like an hour. We were all shaking. When it was over and we looked outside, we saw the whole town was in flames. It looked like a firestorm. Classmates were killed as was the little boy next door, an only child.

Another neighbor was very badly affected by the air raid. The mother went to a nearby bunker and the father and son remained in the house. When the air raid was over, the house was gone and both men had been killed. On the street where I lived, not many homes were left. Most were completely flattened and others were burnt to the ground. Some bombs exploded later. We called them time bombs. It was terrible. Many people were killed that day.

Our town had factories and I guess that is why we were bombed. But, they just didn't target the factories, they bombed everything and everyone. The phosphor bombs they dropped caused the fires. Many Russian girls who had been brought to our town to work in factories were killed. They lived in hastily built temporary housing. Because of all the damage, people had no homes. The Russian girls had been forced to come to Germany to work, but other people came to find work. In 1939, the economy was pretty good and when the war came, help was badly needed.

The store in Remscheid was completely gone but the owners of a flower shop that was still standing allowed us to use a small portion of their place for our goods. Because of the air raid, the manager returned from Russia for a few days and made arrangements to move some of the furniture and merchandise from the Solingen store to the one in Reimscheid.

We had food shortages, too. For a family of three, we were allowed one quarter pound of butter for two weeks, one loaf of bread a week, and many products were not even available. We lived mostly on potatoes. My favorite breakfast is still whole grain German bread and fried potatoes.

Gas lines were cut so fuel was hard to come by. We

had a little stove oven and would gather wood from destroyed homes and any place we could find it. One winter day I met a girl from the building where we had our store. She told me there was some koks (a type of coal) in the basement. So I took some empty potato sacks and climbed through the basement window to take some home on our sledge.

Some air raids occurred in the evening, but sometimes they started in the daytime. One Saturday, after our town had been almost completely destroyed, airplanes started circling over again. My sister was at the police station, but my father (who was not well) and I tried to reach the bunker. We couldn't make it, so we just lay down in the snow. There was so much noise. That was when the town of Solingen was bombed and very little of the town was left.

After the bombing

The manager of our store was at the Russian front. As the German troops were pushed out of Russia, he was killed in Estonia. Many years later I learned he had been buried by the roadside, right where he had fallen.

We had Russian prisoners in our town. After the war, they were released. One of them was walking up the street in front of our apartment house and frightened one of my friends. (She now lives in Connecticut and we have talked on the phone to one another for many years.) The Russian went to our basement and took some suitcases. I ran after him and tried to grab them. I realized he smelled heavily of alcohol. I was very foolish and did not think of the consequence. He pushed a pistol into my chest but I managed to escape and run back into the house. He fired shots into our apartment building and hit a tenant in the ear. The Red Cross car came and took the wounded man to receive medical care. During that period of time, so much vandalism and stealing occurred, mostly by released prisoners and the military. There was also a lot of raping going on, but I was lucky.

It was then that I met a woman on the street who told me her hat shop would be closing and maybe I would like to rent it, which I did. It was a lovely little house, slated on the outside with white trim and green shutters. The shop was in Lennep, famous as the birthplace of Wilhelm Conrad Roentgen, discoverer of the X-ray. Lennep is now part of Remscheid. I had to hire a horse and carriage to move the merchandise to the new store.

Since telephone lines were down and communications were almost impossible, in July of 1945 it was necessary for me to go in person to Wurtenburg to the offices of WMF.

> *A train full of English soldiers passed me. They told me the train was going north and that I should climb in, but after a short while, I had to get out. They wanted to take advantage of me.*

I also visited some friends at the same time. My transportation was in an open wagon attached to a small truck. And this was in the summertime. When I arrived at the house of my friends in Wurtenburg, I was badly sunburned.

At that time there was a great migration of displaced people from different countries, along with many German people. The trip took two days to get to my destination but going home it took six days. I had to make my way the best I could. Most of the time, I walked all day and slept in farmers' barns at night or sometimes in private homes. At one point, a train full of English soldiers passed me. They told me the train was going north and that I should climb in, but after a short while, I had to get out. They wanted to take advantage of me.

Since there weren't many trains in service following the war, I was lucky to finally catch an open-air train, used mostly to transport animals. This train went north and I finally arrived in my hometown.

Along with other displaced persons after the war was a woman teacher who had come from East Prussia. We gave up a room in our apartment to her. Her husband, although not a soldier, was captured by the Russians and held for a number of years before finally being released.

The night before the war ended, artillery shots were heard the whole night long, so we went to the basement. In the morning, we discovered Allied soldiers coming up the street carrying shotguns. They gathered all the German soldiers and some civilians, and marched them for hours and hours to the Rhine valley.

When I think back on those years, I don't know how I survived—really.

Yes, we were happy when the war ended but very sad. There were great food shortages and many Germans starved to death. I was able to exchange for food some pots and pans I could buy from my company. Inflation was terrible. The money my parents had saved was now worth only one-tenth of its real value. I turned every penny over before I spent it.

Germany was once again devastated as it had been after World War I. Those years had been terrible. Food shortages, unemployment, and Nazis and Communists shooting at one another all contributed to the rise of Hitler. At first, in 1939, many Germans thought that he was just acquiring land that had been taken away from us by the Treaty of Versailles. It was a terrible time for all of us.

As for my store, the Lennep location was really only temporary. In 1948, I closed that store and was asked to work in the one in Solingen-Ohligs, which had been opened after the war. I managed that store until it closed in 1952 and then the company offered me a position in bookkeeping and sales in Dusseldorf. I worked there until 1955.

Many of my relatives had come to the United States after World War I. In 1947 they visited us in Germany and they talked my sister and me into also coming. My sister left in 1949, but I was still working and since my father needed help, I stayed at home until after his death in 1953. It then took some time to get my papers together and finish up matters in Germany and at the end of 1955 I traveled to Bremerhaven and then to America. I arrived March 4 and settled in

Glen Rock, New Jersey.

Later I met my husband here in America. His family had lived in East Prussia. When the Russians came into that area, his father escaped by boat to Denmark. My husband, in the military at the time, never saw his father again. Some friends vacationing in Denmark later found the name of my husband's father on a gravestone.

Near the end of the war, my husband had been captured by the Americans and held as a prisoner for about four weeks. He then went to the university and became a design engineer, and shortly thereafter he came to the United States. We were married in West Orange, New Jersey, in 1964.

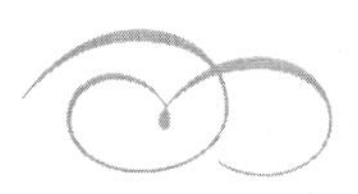

Lilian Williams Abele

Lilian receives great pleasure from knitting, reading, walking, and just being with her "Yank."

Following Germany's horrendous aggression against Poland, Great Britain declared war on Germany September 3, 1939. Many people believed that Hitler's army would immediately cross the English Channel and invade England. But when Neville Chamberlain, our then Prime Minister, came back from Berlin with the agreement promising "peace in our time," a feeling of relief swept the country. But those who had fought in the First World War were not so sure.

I was not yet thirteen years old, had just finished my first year of high school and very proud I was. I was the only one in the whole family ever to go that far in schooling, but many in my family have since gone on to college.

My parents were advised that the school students would be evacuated to the countryside in the event of war and pupils should be equipped as follows: Clothes should be in a knapsack, with gas mask and a packed lunch. Movies often depict parents tearfully waving goodbye to their children, who are all carrying suitcases. In fact, we were not allowed suitcases since it was easier to get around with a backpack and a gas mask over our shoulder.

The school would be evacuated in the event of war and pupils should be equipped as follows: Clothes should be in a knapsack, with gas mask and a packed lunch.

Lilian and George in London

My dad made me a canvas knapsack (nowadays called backpacks) the night before we were due to leave. Parents were not to come to the station—too much confusion. The first day was actually a rehearsal to refine the system, although we didn't know that at the time.

I later learned that the code name for this program was Operation Pied Piper. I don't know how long it ran but I know there were several mass evacuations later in the war.

Over seven hundred schools from the London area took part in that rehearsal and then on the following day, we children left London

Securely locked in our carriages, we noticed that all the signs on the railway stations had been removed, so we had no idea where we were going, and neither did our parents.

for the countryside. This must have been very hard on our parents, though I must admit I don't recall being traumatized in any way.

Securely locked in our carriages, we noticed that all the signs on the railway stations had been removed, so we had no idea where we were going and neither did our parents. We had been issued a postal card to send home once we got settled.

We finally came to a stop at a market town in Norfolk, which was the farthest I had ever been outside London. We were split up and bused to outlying villages. There have been films made where the kindly lady of the manor or the minister's wife, clipboard in hand, leads the children from house to house making sure they are welcomed. This was not so in our case.

We were taken to the local chapel, lined up, and the locals came and chose the girl they decided to house. Ours was an all-girl school so there was no picking a strong kid to help with the farm work, as happened in many cases with the boys. I was always tall and skinny and I felt really bad when I was the only one left in line and there was nobody there to choose me. But finally an older couple came back and said I could share a room with another girl they had already chosen.

So I had a billet, or at least a place to call home, for a while. They were very kind and there were happy times, but I was a city kid, scared to death of the big farm horses, although I loved Mr. Brown, a real gentleman. Early in 1940 I asked to be transferred to another home and was placed with a family at the other end of the village.

All this time Hitler's armies were rampaging through Europe. We in England were mercifully spared the terrors of occupation. One by one the youngsters and some mothers with babies trickled back to London. I was one of them. I didn't like going to school in an old chapel nor did many of us city children really become friends with the village children. We were different and we talked funny. I wrote home and asked to be sent back to London. Surprisingly enough, my father agreed and sent me a ticket. There had been no raids on England and it felt so good to be back in London.

However, I did not return to the old family house, which was a three-story Victorian with high ceilings, wide steps across the front, and iron railings, rather like the New York brownstones I have seen since. The family had moved several districts away since doctors had declared the old neighborhood was not suitable for my sister, who was recovering from rheumatic fever. I was once again in an odd situation, home but not home. I was thirteen years old and now shared a room with my grandmother who had been forced to leave her wonderful overstuffed Victorian furniture when the family moved from an eight-room house to a five-room house.

No schools were open and many weeks passed before the government organized Emergency Secondary Schools, which students attended from many districts. My school was in an area quite far away and involved two bus changes.

Almost immediately, not quite a year from the outbreak of war, the Germans started bombing London. On the 7th of September 1940, over 300 tons of high explosive and incendiary bombs were dropped on the East End, and our old house took a direct hit. We were thankful we were not there. Dozens of warehouses on the docks area were on fire and one fireman was quoted in the newspapers as saying, "It's like the whole bloody world is on fire."

After that attack, bombing was a nightly thing. My sister Pam and I decided to sleep under the stairs knowing that the staircase was usually still intact after a house had been bombed. But sleeping there was too cramped and not very comfortable, so after a few nights, we moved to the floor, placing our heads under the big oak table. That, too, lasted only a few nights. We finally went up to our own beds, each of us praying that we would survive the night.

My journeys to and from school became a daily adventure. Buses could go only so far due to bomb damage. At a certain point we'd have to get off the bus, walk around the damage, and make our way to another bus, if one was running. During the night mobile guns were mounted on the back of army trucks parked on the main street. When they went off it was a terrific noise but nobody minded since we thought they were protecting us. After the war it was said they were of little or no value as far as hitting any bombers but they certainly did wonders for the morale of the local people.

On December 30, all hell broke loose over London. One hundred and thirty-six planes dropped over 22,000 firebombs, and London was indeed ablaze. Over 3,000 people died and 5,000 were seriously wounded. And the bombings continued night after night after night.

Some of our neighbors went every night with their bundles of blankets and personal items down into the Tube, London's underground railway system. By the end of January there was a sort of society down there and soon bunk beds were lining the walls of the stations. Badly needed sanitary facilities were set up. My parents decided if we were to die, we would be at home, not underground. My brother had joined the army and was away.

We had a few weeks respite when Hitler concentrated on the shipping convoys and the port cities, but the bombing started up again. It was then that Buckingham Palace, home of our King and Queen, was damaged.

I watched rescuers pull body after body from the basement shelters. People had died not only from the building collapsing, but the gas lines had ruptured, and the water mains had burst.

I remember going to school one day through an area with many large blocks of flats (apartments). We'd had a terrible raid the previous night and my mother did not want me to go to school, but I did. Along with other people, I watched rescuers pull body after body from the basement shelters. People had died not only from the building collapsing, but the gas lines had ruptured and the water mains had burst. It was a sight I will never forget. This scene was brought back in horror when I watched the rescue attempts following the September 11 attacks in New York.

Five hundred bombers hit London one night. Can you imagine the damage? And the industrial cities in the midlands were being pounded, also. But by now the Royal Air Force was bombing Germany with great success, or at least that's what the newspapers told us. Suddenly the hierarchy of the church started wondering out loud about the "immoral raids" we were making on towns in Germany. Certainly Londoners and other bomb victims were all for the bombing. We had had it long enough.

By May 1944, England was full of troops from all

During the day raids, our office staff had to go down to the basement shelter under the building, each of us carrying our typewriter and the projects we were working on.

over the world preparing for D-Day. It was a standing joke that the barrage balloons, which were to stop low flying aircraft, were the only things holding up our little island.

I had graduated and was working in the city. Soon after D-Day I recall hearing and then seeing a strange plane flying overhead. Most of us recognized our fighters and bombers but this one had a strange sound. Suddenly the engine stopped. People I have spoken to since all agree with me that we thought the pilot was in trouble, and if he didn't soon eject he would go down with the plane.

The new plane was a V-1. We called them Doodlebugs or Buzzbombs because of the droning noise they made before they cut out. Each one would flatten about a quarter mile radius and we quickly learned to wait for the silence and then duck for cover. The first ones fell on my old neighborhood, which had been so badly hit early in the war.

During the day raids, our office staff had to go down to the basement shelter under the building, each of us carrying our typewriter and the projects we were working on. There we stayed until the attack ended.

By the beginning of September, while our armies were pushing forward into Europe, we had a new enemy, the V-2 rocket, a truly terrifying enemy. We couldn't hear these rockets coming, just a tremendous explosion followed by a strange whooshing sound (they were flying faster than the speed of sound) and they were the worst of the lot. We simply had no warning. But we still went to the pictures (movies) and danced and skated and had wonderful parties when friends came home on leave. At our age we were invincible.

During the last year of the war and also the following year, I volunteered on weekends at a British servicemen's canteen in the West End (downtown, as Americans would call it). Also, I was old enough to join the Air Raid Precautions as a messenger, running a route between the Report Center where calls came in about unexploded bombs and damage done, and the Control Center where the fire brigade and ambulance brigade were alerted. It was a short distance between the two buildings, but it was upsetting one night to learn that incendiary bombs had been dropped along my street. Fortunately, every house had two buckets on the front step, one filled with water and one filled with sand, which were put to good use that night. But our neighbor complained bitterly the next day that his prize tulip bed had been violated, even though the dirt from his garden was needed to put out the many small fires. Nobody ever told him who the culprit was.

We had food rationing, of course. My mother lined up each morning at the local shops to get what she could. We never went hungry since mothers have a way of stretching what they have into wonderful stews, still my favorite food.

Roller skating was very popular. We had all skated in the streets since we were old enough to walk, it seemed, and almost every night we would go either to the pictures or to Alexandra Palace a couple of miles away. This was, as the name implies, a wonderful Edwardian pleasure palace set high on a hill in a grand park setting. Can you imagine a ballroom big enough to convert to a full size skating rink? We loved it and no matter what was going on outside, hundreds of young people congregated there for an evening of fun, music and skating. It was here that I first met a young American soldier,

George Abele. He was eighteen and I was seventeen. We were together at the Palace every evening for the rest of his furlough. He was part of a U. S. anti-aircraft battalion attached to the British army in the defense of London.

During the Battle of the Bulge there was no mail for many weeks. George and I had been writing regularly and when his letters stopped coming, my mother hoped that our romance had ended. None of us knew about the battle being fought in the Ardennes, so when the mail finally arrived, I know Mother was more than a little disappointed.

V-E Day arrived when I was eighteen years old, too young according to my mother to go into the West End for the celebrations. However I was allowed to go to the final Victory Parade after V-J Day.

George was back in the United States and we were corresponding regularly, hoping that I could join him shortly. Finally I received my visa enabling me to come to America to marry George. But I had no transportation. At last he was able to secure a ticket for me to Philadelphia and we were married in October 1947. At our wedding the best man jokingly said, "I'll give it a year and she'll be back in England." Well, I'm still here.

My grandfather served Queen Victoria in the African campaign known as the Boer War. My father served in the First World War, was taken prisoner and suffered greatly in POW camps. Two of his brothers had already been killed on the battlefield. His younger brother, too young for that war, was called up in World War II and served with the Royal Artillery in North Africa against Rommel. Torpedoed and rescued at sea, he would never again set foot in a boat of any size until the day he died at a great age in December 2001. My brother served in the Far East and knows well the area of Afghanistan and the caves where our troops are today searching for Bin Laden. He serviced small arms that were then dropped by parachute to the freedom fighters in Europe. Our middle son joined the U.S. Army upon graduation from high school, served his enlistment and remained an active reservist. He was recalled to duty and served another eighteen months, one year in Operation Iraqi Freedom. Each generation, through no fault of their own, has been involved in this barbaric occupation we call War.

Me? When I became an American citizen, the presiding judge admonished the group saying, "Understand this, you are not Anglo-American, Italian-American, or German-American. You are now American!" And I am one proud American.

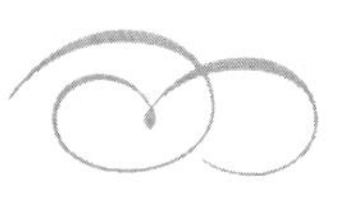

Marion York Anderson

Marion spent her childhood in Chiswick, West London, where she attended the Hogarth School. The war years found her falling in love with an American, an adventure that led to a lifelong love affair with America.

Rememberings 1939-1945

When I was born
The midwife said to Mummie
"You were the seventh
She's the seventh
Carried for seven
And born at seven.
She'll be the lucky one, she will."

But, the 30s were hard
And then came Hitler.
Six years—all teenage ones
Filled with experiences
Undreamed of.
On hindsight they are memories
That bring tears and laughter
In proportion
And none regretted.

The first big jolt came
When I was sent to the country
With the school.

Marion at age 12

Mummie insisted I needed to learn
But, being twelve
I thought I knew
Just about everything.

Desperately homesick then
And almost two years later
I returned to London—grown
I tiptoed through the dark streets
And began living with air raid sirens
Bombs and fires
Barrage balloons and doodlebugs.
All the time, carrying my gas mask.

But, I was home
And best of all—in the thick of it.
Sirens, soldiers, rations, darkness.
Windows dark, street lamps dark
No traffic
No traffic lights
Only the sound of people
Quickly walking home
Before the raids begin.

Then I remember
Standing with my father
Above the air raid shelter
Sharing his cigarette with me.
At fourteen I was feeling
Twentv-four.
Too grown up now to be
Down in the shelter
With the babies and my mother
Nursing the cat.

Home was now a strange place.
Always the familiar brown paint
Evident color of mixed leftovers.
Daddy the local contractor
Successful second generation
Now crippled by war.
Who wants to decorate?
Who wants to repair or improve?
No one.

Mummie didn't get cross much
But she did insist
Our windows get replaced.
Blown out twice
And then again
No plywood for her.
It was enough to suffer
Black curtains and forty watt bulbs.
So much pride in Daddy's reputation
And so much effort
In trying to carry on.

There were many difficult nights
And many mornings of anxiety.
Cheers when it was all still there
And happy cups of tea
In celebration.
Another night Hitler didn't get us
But then always wondering
About the others
And waiting for some word.

One early dawn
Mary grabbed my hand
And we set off to Woolsley Gardens.
A stick of eight had dropped close by
And we had to see what happened.
It was still dark
And we were walking fast.
A bobby stopped us and warned
"Careful lass,
Lots of horseflesh about."
The dairy stables had been hit.

Terrified, we rushed to Auntie Connie's house
To find them without a roof
Sitting by the fire
In hats and coats
Drinking gin from a teapot.
We sat with them
We too drank gin
Remembering those lovely horses
That had delivered our milk
Everyday.

We walked home
Past the house we all grew up in
Vacated two years before
But now a pile of rubble.
It was nearly morning
We walked back
A couple of girls—giggling from the gin.
Mary said "Let's go home
To our own beds.
Not to the shelter
To hell with Hitler."
And we did.

So it went. The war wore on.
But to our salvation
And our delight
The Americans had come to England.
So happy, so kind, so friendly
On twenty-four hours leave in London
Giving us brief glimpses
Of this amazing U.S. invasion.

The Yanks soon began
The daytime strikes on Hitler
And we would cheer
As those enormous planes
Took off on our behalf across London.
And we would weep
About teatime
When the crippled ones
Struggled to make a landing
On their return.

Rations were now really slim
We hadn't seen a banana
Or an orange
For four years
And the grocerman was doing his bit
By careful measurement
Of every ounce of butter
Every ounce of tea
Every ounce of cheese
And apologizing
For giving us two cracked eggs again.
As usual, we'd say,
"Never mind."

One day an American boy
Came into our family.
Bill had met him
While taking pictures
Of the church steeple in High Wycombe.
He would cycle thirty miles to visit
Fearless, energetic, all American.
He would appear in the garden
And call out that he was there.
Bill would throw down the key
And another short sweet visit
Was had by all.

One summer day Bill heard that call
Looked out the window and as usual
Raised it quickly
But, it was tomato time
And a row of ripe tomatoes
Were sitting on the windowsill.
Have you ever seen
Ten squashed tomatoes
Running down a windowpane?
We did laugh.

And the war went on some more.
Now confident
And seventeen
When I wasn't working
I was at the movies
If not at the movies,
I was dancing.

Dancing with the few males left
The Conscientious Objectors
Conscripted into the bomb squad
In every neighbourhood.
They were magnificent and brave
Detonating everything
To keep us safe.

By now, everyone had left home but me.
And for the first time
It was quiet.
The raids had stopped.
Hitler was broken.
We celebrated V-E Day
Then V-J Day
And then the Americans left.

One sunny morning that summer
Mummie was washing the dishes
Looking out the window
To the garden.
"Oh my goodness—look," she said.
The air raid shelter that Daddy had built
With cots and chairs
Wireless and books
Had suddenly sunk
Into a big hole.

That shelter had been such comfort
During the daytime raids
And looked beautiful too
With gorgeous red geraniums on top.
But it was all gone
Disappeared in a second.
And Mummie and I fell into stitches
Of laughter
"What timing," we said
God works in wondrous ways.
The war was over.

MOTHERS
Send them out
of London
Give them a chance of greater safety and health

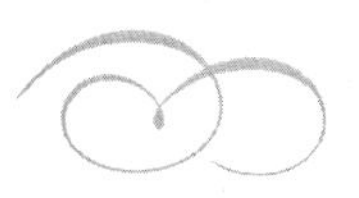

Helen Stawicki Schneider

Helen and her husband, both retired, live in Chillicothe, Illinois. They enjoy time with their grandchildren, their son and his wife, traveling in their R.V. and spending winters in south Texas.

Excerpted from a family memoir written by Helen Schneider and shared by her sister Barbara Stawicki Anniballi of Doylestown, PA.

World War II began in 1939 when Germany invaded Poland, but for us in the deep parts of Poland, very little changed. Life was peaceful and calm, except for incidents of violence we heard about occasionally when German troops went through villages en route to the big cities. We lived in Dobra, in the center of Poland, about 125 miles southwest of Warsaw. My father, Stanley Stawicki, was a school principal and my mother, Alicia, a part-time teacher.

It was in August of 1941 when war came to our family. We were visiting my paternal grandparents in Slesin. We had finished dinner and my mother and Aunt Maria were helping Grandma clean up in the kitchen. Dad and I were going through the big garden down to the bottom of the field for a swim in the river. When we arrived at the tomato field, a plane went over us. We stood staring at it, and then it turned around and came back towards us.

When we arrived at the tomato field, a plane went over us. We stood staring at it, and then it turned around and came back towards us.

Helen, Gram, and Barbara

Dad, who was a few feet ahead of me, seemed to fly through the air, knocking me down into all those old rotten tomatoes and threw himself on top of me as machine gun fire exploded all around us. To this day I can see the pointing machine gun sticking out of that huge plane spitting those red long bullets at us. As we hid in the tomato plants the plane seemed so low that it appeared as if it was going to hit the farmhouse.

That same evening while a lot of villagers were still

Dad and a few other men were lined up against the schoolhouse wall as traitors to be shot.

mingling on the road in front of the house, three Gestapo officers came riding into the front drive. Mother and the kids ran into the yard behind the house. After awhile my grandfather came into the house and said that they were taking the three men to the old school house for a meeting. Years later I learned from my father that the villagers were going to kill the Germans, thinking they would never be missed. But my father explained to the others that someone would check on their whereabouts, which would cause dire consequences for the village.

We left for home the next day and never saw our paternal grandparents again. Life was completely different from then on. The German soldiers arrived in our village, closing the church and converting the school into a military compound. Since Dad could speak German, he was told by the Germans to work in the town hall.

Everything changed. A 7 p.m. curfew was imposed. If you had to be out after that hour you needed a pass from the police station. Restaurants in Dobra were only open to German soldiers and German families. The German families were brought in to take over all the Jewish-owned businesses, after the Jews were taken away. Ration and ID cards were given out to every family and no matter where we went we had to have the cards with us. All the college-educated people and all the Jews had to register at the town hall and report weekly to the commandant.

German soldier patrols and Gestapo motorcycles came through the streets frequently during the day, sometimes stopping at homes and walking through or asking to be fed. If they'd see a few kids playing together it was a ritual that they'd stop and teach us how to salute Heil-Hitler style. They would make us march into our homes as they watched us salute our parents and tell them to do the same.

Of course, all the kids loved to salute and we did so constantly. But when I was called into the house for lunch one day and enthusiastically saluted Mother while she was at the sink doing dishes, I got a wet dishcloth slapped across my face. I was told in no uncertain terms never to do that again unless a German was watching.

One fall day a man came running to Mother about a disturbance at the school courtyard. Mother rushed out of the house with me right behind her. Dad and a few other men were lined up against the schoolhouse wall as traitors to be shot. On occasion when the Germans encountered some opposition from the Polish people, they would pick a few men at random who were looked up to in the community and execute them as examples so that no one would dare oppose the German Reich. As Mother tried to get through the soldiers to reach Dad, a man in black came up and pulled Dad from the line. It was one of the Gestapo officers that Dad had saved from death a couple of years before in the incident at Slesin.

In March of 1943 Dad came home early one day telling us that he had to be in the city in two days to board a train for Germany. He was being sent to a German work camp. The following morning the whole family walked with Dad to the train, filled with men and their families. The men were all teachers or engineers.

About a month after Dad left, the commandant brought a newspaper from Germany showing a bombed train all in splinters and he told us that Dad was killed by the Americans during an air strike. After he left, Mother told me not to cry. She had heard from the underground that Dad was alive and on his way to France to join the underground fighters.

"But if someone asks you about your father," she said, "you bite your tongue or pinch yourself real hard and cry like hell, as if you really lost your father, and I'll do the same."

Mother was pregnant when Dad left, but I didn't know until later. For me the news of a baby coming sounded great, but Mother would cry often. Neighboring farmers would bring milk and butter for us so we didn't have to stand in line at the stores for our rations. The summer of 1943 was lonely for us. Mother wouldn't leave the house and I was not allowed out of her sight. The wife of one of the farmers came to visit quite often and she was the one who delivered my baby sister Barbara on September 29, 1943.

One Sunday in the fall of 1943 we had a special treat. Mother said we were going to the park. We dressed Barbara like a little doll and put her in my old carriage. While walking in the park Mother told me that we would meet a lady and a man with news of Dad. Mother said we won't know them, but we'll pretend like they are old friends and I should call them Aunt and Uncle when we greet them.

That's what we did and we all acted like old friends. They brought candy for me, and the man said that Dad was to tell Ali Halina (my name in Poland) and Barbara that he loves us and he is okay. The people did not know where he was since this was all the information they managed to obtain through the underground radio.

Helen's father (left)

Another evening the commandant came to our house. He told us to be ready at a moment's notice to be moved out of our area. We would only be allowed one bag of clothing and one bag of food to take with us. Loudspeakers blasted day and night for people to get ready to leave or be slaughtered by the Russians. Wagon trains carrying refugees was a never-ending sight.

In early January of 1944, there was a banging and yelling at our door. The Germans told Mother they needed our house for their headquarters and we should be out of there within an hour and into a wagon train. The farmer across the street, who also was told to get out, sent us a wagon and a man to drive us.

Mother always carried a big brown bag with her. She told me I would have to help her guard it if we ever had to get out fast. In it she had important papers, some of her good jewelry in special little compartments and photos of our last Christmas. She said that if we would run out of money she could sell the jewelry

"If someone asks you about your father," she said, "you bite your tongue or pinch yourself real hard and cry like hell, as if you really lost your father."

Every so often we would see a wagon and its horses in a ravine, the horses' legs broken and the wagons all smashed having slid off the icy road.

for money in return for food, which we did have to do when we reached Germany.

Mother grabbed up rolls, cookies, a kielbasa sausage, and a big can of milk from the farmer. I had a doll and a few books all ready to take with me but mother said I needed to hold Barb. That was the end of our living in Dobra.

Thus began our long journey by wagon train. It snowed and snowed and snowed. Every so often we would see a wagon and its horses in a ravine, the horses' legs broken and the wagons all smashed having slid off the icy road. We did everything in our wagon—slept, ate, sang songs, and told stories.

At dusk we would arrive at a town with just a few little lights blinking and the smell of smoke coming from house chimneys. It reminded us that there were people still living in their homes. Finally we came into farm country—after being on the road forever, it seemed to me, but Ma said it was only about a week. That was when the wagon commandant came around and divided the wagon train into sections.

One section went to a school to spend the night and the other section was accommodated at neighboring farms. If we went to the school, we had desks to sit at when we ate. The German soldiers would provide bread and rolls and watermilk for the kids and we slept on straw mattresses on the floor. If we went to a farm, the accommodations were in the stables or barns. Even though the powerful animal smell of cows was bad at times, I liked it better when we stopped at the farms because sleeping with the animals kept us warmer. The farm people treated us kindly and I would play with the kids, but for only a little while.

The closer we got to Berlin, the louder the bombing and artillery fire became. In the city of Berlin, the ruins were monstrous. On the north of Berlin, the bombing became even more frequent and often we would have to scramble into ditches and hide in the trees.

One day we were told that we could go no farther because the highways were all bombed and under repair. As we rode along the suburbs of Potsdam, we saw people making their homes in bombed out buildings and houses. At one point, we saw a couple of ladies standing looking at us when our wagons happened to stop in front of them. They came over and asked where we were from. Ma spoke with them for a while and then they said they had one room in their house that we could use, if we could manage to share a bathroom with all of the other occupants in the house. When we were settled in that evening, Ma said, "Halina, tonight we can talk to the Lord in private."

The German ladies shared food with us since they were allowed more rations at the market because they had us in their house. We ate picnic style and it was great sitting at a table eating different kinds of food. I loved being in a home again, even though it was only one room. The ladies went shopping and came back with fresh bread, carrots, potatoes, and bones from the black market. It smelled so good when Ma made a big tub of soup.

I had hoped we could stay there forever since it was the closest thing to home we had ever had, but we had to get back on the wagon train after a week or so. The air raids and the wailing sirens were almost constant. The wagonmaster told us that our section of the train was being sent to the farming region.

Ma began teaching me how to cope with the baby while she would be in the field. We were directed to a farm in Schladen, Germany, its owner being an older widow, Frau Bunze. She had one other family already on the farm and she said she picked us from the list she received from the wagon-master because Ma spoke German. The other people were Austrian and had two kids younger than me.

Frau Bunze was very good to us. While Ma was in the sheds working, preparing potatoes and turnips ready for planting, Frau Bunze would come to check on Barb and me in our room upstairs. She would bring eggs, milk and sometimes a little square of butter. Ma was allowed to bring some potatoes home with her too, so we ate good.

As spring 1945 approached things became worse. The fields around the farmhouse were full of German soldiers, tanks, and heavy machine guns. The rumor was that the field beyond the farmhouse was to be the battlefield. No one was allowed outside and the sound of gunfire kept coming closer. Sometimes it sounded as if the bullets came right through the attic above us.

One morning in April of 1945, Ma woke me and told me to get dressed. She thought something would be happening out in the field. Artillery guns were going off and bombs were dropping. Frau Bunze came to tell us to come down to the cellar. After a long time everything went quiet.

Liberation by the American and British armies

Ma ran upstairs to get something for the baby and when she came back she said the field was full of dead soldiers. We stayed in the cellar until the following morning when a man from the village banged on all the doors and windows yelling, "The Americans and English and their tanks are all over the village." We could see the big tanks and jeeps driving up and down all the roads, sometimes driving across the fields looking for soldiers still in hiding. We kids would run to the gate and look to see if they looked different from us. Then they would drive up to us and pass out chocolate bars, candy, and crackerjack.

Ma ran upstairs to get something for the baby and when she came back she said the field was full of dead soldiers.

We had to go into the village and register. The Americans and British Red Cross were also there to help with food and clothing. Ma told them that we had a grandmother and aunts who also were brought out of Poland to Germany.

A couple months later, two uniformed ladies came to see Ma. They

I was so out of breath that I was gasping as I told her, "Daddy is looking for us from England!"

had found Grandma, my mother's mother Emma Berendt, and my aunts Tillie and Natalie Berendt living in the next town over from us. It was a happy day when, after confirming that we were family, the two Red Cross officers brought Gram, Tillie, and Natalie to us. After a few weeks Ma asked Frau Bunze to let Gram, Tillie, and Natalie move in with us. She agreed and they worked for her in the milk house.

Shortly after that, the Red Cross ladies (who said they were Quakers) came again and offered Mother and Natalie jobs in the Displaced Persons (DP) camp in Vienenburg am Hartz. Mother would be a teacher and Natalie a nurse, but we would have to move. We hated to leave Frau Bunze because she had become a good friend. But I was excited because we were going to have our own place again and I was going back to school like a regular kid.

So it came about that we were part of a family again and had what we called a home. Life seemed to be going pretty well and I enjoyed school and having friends to play with again. Ma made sure that we remembered Dad in our prayers every day. We hoped we would find him through the Red Cross, just like we found the rest of our family. I was busy all day. School for me ended at noon, then I went for piano lessons, Girl Scout meetings, and basketball practice, and on my free afternoons I helped Natalie at the child daycare room.

While tuning the radio one day at lunchtime, I heard the BBC/Red Cross come in real clear with a voice saying that Stanley Stawicki stationed in England with the British-Allied Forces is looking for the whereabouts of his wife Alicja, daughter Halina and a baby daughter Barbara. If anyone has seen or heard of them, please contact the English Red Cross station in Vienenburg.

That day I didn't care about lunch. Gram was crying and Tillie kept calling, "Wait for me," as I took off running. I didn't stop till I was in front of Ma. I was so out of breath that I was gasping as I told her, "Daddy is looking for us from England." I thought she didn't hear me because she just stared at me and sat back down. I kept telling her, "Come on Ma, we have to go and make a phone call to the Red Cross." She made me repeat what I had said about three times.

Ma canceled classes that day and the next day while arrangements were being made by one of the officers for us to talk to Dad on the radio through the military. Ma was the only one that could speak with him and for only a few minutes. It wasn't till early spring of 1946 that Dad was allowed to come see us.

When he finally came he was in uniform, a lieutenant with the Allied Forces stationed in Inverary, Scotland. During the course of his visit, we learned that the train on which he had been traveling when he left Poland had been bombed, and during the commotion, Dad and three other men from our area took off into the dark. They headed for the countryside, came upon more men in hiding, and together walked at night until finally arriving in France. There, they encountered English spies who asked them to join the Allied Forces. Along with other men just like them who had escaped from the Nazis, they were trained to participate in D-Day, the invasion of Normandy.

Dad had only one week with us and we loved having him back. Before he left, Grandma who always enjoyed chit-chatting with Dad, told him that she wanted to come with us to Scotland to be with her grandchildren. Dad promised to start her paperwork as soon as permissible after he had us settled in housing.

Tillie decided to stay in Germany for awhile and try to get together with Musyj, her fiancé, who we learned was at another DP camp. They planned to marry and emigrate to America where Tillie was corresponding with a distant relative. Natalie, who still wanted to see some of the world, decided to accept an offer to be a nurse on a ship that carried emigrants to various countries, but eventually she settled in the United States and became a governess in New Jersey.

Displaced Persons camp in Vienenburg

When we finally arrived in Scotland, Dad had a couple of rooms rented for us at Pennymore Farm on the outskirts of Furnace, Argyllshire. One of the farm families had a daughter Chrissie my age. We were together all the time. Weekends were special when we were allowed to roam the fields covered in blankets of yellow daffodils and purple heather. We would bring armfuls of flowers home to our mothers and help Chrissie's father plant potatoes in the field along Loch Fyne. In the summers we went swimming off the big rocks jutting out of the Loch at low tide and gathered up seaweed to dry for making bonfires in the evenings when our parents walked on the beach with us.

We all loved living in Scotland until Gram died and again we were without family. Since both Tillie and Natalie had decided to settle in the United States, our family made the same decision when Dad was demobilized and given an opportunity to choose where he wanted to live.

And so it was on October 21, 1951 at 8:00 a.m., we boarded the Queen Elizabeth at Southampton, England for our trip to New York, and to our new life in the United States.

Also by Peg George:

"This semi-autobiographical recounting of one woman's endeavor to survive in the men's club of local politics ***tells it like it is.****"*

A trailblazer recalls her political journey

$14.95
To order or inquire about speaking engagements:
Margaret Hewitt George
133 Progress Drive
Doylestown, PA 18901
215-345-0522
www.PegGeorge.com

"Clearly written in the form of a journal starting in 1970, *Never Use Your Dim Lights* describes the sometimes not too pretty realities of the rough and tumble of life in the People's House. Sometimes up, often down, she can still say at the denouement of her pilgrimage, 'I wouldn't have missed it for the world.' While the names and places have been changed, for anyone who wants to understand the machinations of Pennsylvania politics, this is a must read."

—H. William DeWeese, Minority Leader Pennsylvania House of Representatives.